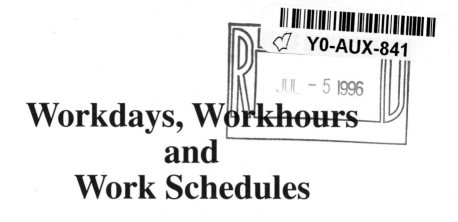

Workdays, Workhours
and
Work Schedules

Evidence for the United States and Germany

Daniel S. Hamermesh
University of Texas at Austin

1996

W.E. Upjohn Institute for Employment Research
Kalamazoo, Michigan

Library of Congress Cataloging-in-Publication Data

Hamermesh, Daniel S.
  Workdays, workhours, and work schedules : evidence for the United
States and Germany / Daniel S. Hamermesh..
    p. cm.
  Includes bibliographical references and index.
  ISBN 0–88099–169–0 (paper : alk. paper). — ISBN 0–88099–170–4
(cloth : alk. paper)
  1. Hours of labor—United States. 2. Hours of labor—Germany.
3. Workweek—United States. 4. Workweek—Germany. 5. Part-time
employment—United States. Part-time employment—Germany.
I. Title.
HD5124.H35   1996
331.25'7'0973—dc20   96–11199
                                                                         CIP

Copyright © 1996
W. E. Upjohn Institute for Employment Research
300 S. Westnedge Avenue
Kalamazoo, Michigan 49007–4686

The facts presented in this study and the observations and viewpoints expressed are the sole responsibility of the author. They do not necessarily represent positions of the W. E. Upjohn Institute for Employment Research.

Cover design by J. R. Underhill
Index prepared by Shirley Kessel.
Printed in the United States of America.

Acknowledgments

I thank the Bureau of Labor Statistics for providing the American data in an easily usable fashion. The German data used in this study are from the public-use version of the German Socioeconomic Panel study. They were provided by the Deutsches Institut für Wirtschaftsforschung, and were made especially accessible to me by Richard Burkhauser of Syracuse University and Gert Wagner of the DIW. They and their staffs made a foreign data set particularly easy to use by someone who had not previously been familiar with this survey. Jeremy Ben-Israel and Marcelo Tamez were instrumental in getting these data sets into shape so that I could perform the necessary statistical analyses.

My colleagues Melissa Famulari and Gerald Oettinger offered numerous suggestions on early drafts of various chapters, as did Brock Blomberg, Richard Blundell, Richard Freeman, Knut Gerlach, Jean Kimmel, Katharina Spiess and John Treble. I am especially indebted to Bob Hart, John Owen and Ronald Schettkat, who read the entire manuscript for the Institute and offered detailed and very useful general and specific comments. Participants at seminars at Universität Hannover, University College London, Syracuse University, the University of Texas at Austin, the University of Texas at Dallas and Vanderbilt University, and at the National Bureau of Economic Research, the Deutsches Institut für Wirtschaftsforschung, the Conference on Labor Demand of the University of Aarhus, the Tinbergen Institute in Amsterdam, the Board of Governors of the Federal Reserve, the Federal Reserve Bank of New York, and the Milken Institute offered helpful comments too. The international perspective provided by comments received at several of these institutions was a useful antidote to the ethnocentrism of someone whose previous work had concentrated on the U.S. labor market. I benefited profoundly from comments received during a seminar at the Upjohn Institute and at several stages during the research.

Most important, the manuscript benefited throughout, as has all my scholarly work, from the encouragement, good sense and terrific intuition of my wife, Frances Hamermesh, to whom this work is dedicated.

Author

Daniel S. Hamermesh is the Edward Everett Hale Centennial professor of economics at the University of Texas at Austin and research associate at the National Bureau of Economic Research. He received his Ph.D. from Yale University in 1969 and taught at Princeton and Michigan State Universities. He has published books and journal articles in a variety of areas of labor market analysis and is the author of *Labor Demand* (Princeton University Press, 1993).

CONTENTS

LIST OF TABLES

LIST OF FIGURES

CHAPTER 1

Setting the Stage

The Main Issues

The use of time is central among the decisions people make throughout their lives. These decisions include choices about time spent on the job as well as time spent at home. Not surprisingly, the ubiquity of time use decisions in people's lives has been matched by their pervasiveness in the body of research that labor economists have undertaken. They have been the focus of two major areas of labor economics, studies of labor supply and of labor demand.

There are two distinct ways of analyzing people's utilization of their available time: *integrally*, by how time is allocated into separate activities over some relatively long time interval; and *instantaneously*, by which few (one, or at most several) of the myriad possible activities are engaged in at a particular point in time. The general issue in the study of time use is whether we add up (integrate) people's activities over some longer period of time or instead take snapshots of what they are doing at particular points in time (instantaneously).

For nearly fifty years most of our data have been collected and presented in ways that make studying the integral use of time fairly easy. For example, the American Current Population Survey (CPS)-style data generate information about total activity during the past week. Even within this integral approach to time use the choice of temporal aggregates has been remarkably restrictive. Stimulated by the availability of CPS-type data, we have devoted tremendous attention to hours of work and leisure integrated over the week. Information obtained retrospectively (e.g., from the CPS, the Census, or the annual surveys that make up our large panels of household data) has allowed some analysis of weeks of work integrated over the (previous) year; and in some cases this has been combined with the study of (current) weekly hours. We have paid some attention to integrating time use over the lifetime (though generally through the construction of artificial life histories). Other potentially interesting possibilities, such as integrating over the day to examine daily hours of work and nonmarket activities or integrating over the week to obtain days of work, have been generally ignored by economists and studied only very sparsely by other researchers.

Most sets of data do not allow one to study instantaneous time use. Even where such data are available, however, we integrate the information into categories that mirror those available in standard data sets, so that we lose their underlying instantaneous characteristics.[1] Because of these problems and choices, instantaneous time use has received much less attention than integral time use.

The central purpose and overarching theme of this monograph are its move beyond standard approaches to studying time use to see what we can learn from other ways of looking at the data. The two major new foci are: (1) the division of work time into hours per day and days per week (as opposed to the standard analysis of weekly hours of work), a novel integration of time use; and (2) the patterns of the particular times of the day and week when people are working, a focus on instantaneous time use. The novelty of the approach should itself generate interesting insights into how people spend their time and how those outcomes differ across groups in the population. If nothing else, these will enhance our understanding of what the standard cuts of the data have been telling us.

These approaches can do more than that, however. By analyzing workers' and employers' choices of workdays and working hours per day, we will be able to understand the role of fixed costs of getting to work and of adding workdays to plant schedules in a way that enhances our understanding of the relation between work time and the determination of employment. This in turn has implications for a variety of government policies, including those that offer incentives to alter work schedules or that attempt to offset the costs of working. Thus policies on overtime work and the length of workdays and workweeks require the analysis in this monograph, as indeed does any policy related to the restructuring of time at work. Similarly, additional light can be shed on policies related to child care if we can learn more about how the length of the workday is determined and how people time their working hours over the day and week.

An International Perspective

Most of the detailed analyses presented in this monograph are carried out using microeconomic data for both the United States and Germany (actually, the previous West Germany only). I study two economies rather than the usual one for two reasons. First, and most important, all too often the ethnocentric focus of American social scientists on facts that are country-specific detracts from their ability to provide generally useful results and to tell whether tests of their theories have anything more than parochial applications. A bit broader focus is a wonderful check on our tendency to generalize findings from what may be the unique and idiosyncratic socioeconomic outcomes produced by tastes, policies, institutions and temporary aberrations in our own country. A second justification is that the detailed study of two countries' outcomes along narrow dimensions allows us to use conclusions about behavior in each to examine the impact of the other country's policies.

I choose to study Germany for several reasons. Like the United States, it is a large industrialized economy. Yet it is sufficiently different socially from the United States to generate some interesting comparisons. Also, it is the only such country for which an easily accessible set of data is available that provides information on days, daily hours and work schedules on a broad sample of workers that is more or less comparable to U.S. data, but that also complements them in various ways.

As background information for those comparisons, consider first the information on broad labor-market outcomes shown for 1991 in the United States (1990 in the former West Germany) presented in table 1.1. Whether we use the official data or attempt to make the data more comparable by calculating labor force participation from the samples used in this study, it is quite clear that female participation in the former West Germany is substantially below that in the United States (and is in fact comparable to female participation in the United States in the late 1970s).

By 1990 average weekly hours of work in Germany were lower than in the United States. Other evidence shows that they are also much more tightly distributed around this average. Very few German workers

are working extremely long hours (see Hamermesh 1995); and, as the
table shows, a smaller fraction of the German labor force was on part-
time schedules, despite the fact that part-time work is defined as 34
hours or less in the United States, but 36 hours or less in Germany
(where in some industries 36 hours is the standard workweek). A long-
time American citizen born in Germany summed up the difference in
workers' attitudes toward labor supply by noting that, "Germans put
leisure first and work second. In America, it's the other way around."[2]

**Table 1.1   Labor Market Characteristics, United States, 1991,
and Germany, 1990**

	United States	Germany
Female participation rate:		
All women ≥ 17[a]	53.2	45.4
Women ages 17-64[a]	63.4	52.9
Official[b]	57.4	52.0
Average weekly work hours[b]	39.3	38.3
Percent part-time workers[b]	18.9	15.0
Percent self-employed[c]	7.6	7.7
Percent with second jobs[a]	6.6	7.2
Unionization (percentages in 1990)[d]	15.6	32.9
Unemployment rate[b]	6.6	7.2

a. Calculated from the May 1991 CPS and the GSOEP.
b. Taken from *Employment and Earnings*, January 1992, and from Institut für Arbeitsmarkt- und
Berufsforschung, *Zahlen-Fibel*, 1992. The U.S. participation rate covers all women ages 16 and
over; the German rate covers women 15 through 65.
c. OECD, *Employment Outlook*, July 1992, p.158.
d. OECD, *Employment Outlook,* July 1994, p. 184.

The rate of self-employment is almost identical in the two countries,
as measured in the most comparable way. That measurement, however,
excludes owner-managers of incorporated enterprises, so that it is
likely that the incidence is somewhat higher in the United States than
in Germany, though the differences are probably not large. The comparisons in the table, which are based on similar sets of household

interviews, suggest that moonlighting rates are quite similar in the two countries. When we eliminate short second jobs (less than 20 hours per week), those that are unlikely to affect the worker's typical daily hours, total workdays per week or timing of work on a typical day, we find that the incidence is quite low in both countries, though it is much higher in the United States (1.9 percent) than in Germany (0.3 percent).

The biggest international difference is in the incidence of unionization, which is over twice as great in Germany as in the United States and, in contrast to the American decline, has been relatively stable over the past two decades. Moreover, union contracts in many German industries are formally extended to nonunion plants, a phenomenon that (at least explicitly) is very rare in the United States. These differences mean that any international similarities that we find are all the more striking, since they arise out of labor markets that differ substantially along this one dimension.

Aggregate unemployment in the two countries was quite similar in these two years, so that in the comparisons in the following chapters we are examining labor markets that are at roughly the same degree of tightness. We should remember, however, that for the United States the 6.6 percent represents experience during the middle of a long but moderate recession. The German unemployment rate of 7.2 percent marked the fifth and penultimate year of falling unemployment.

The industrial structures of the two countries also differ, as shown by the data in table 1.2 on the distributions of employment by industry. The U.S. workforce is much less concentrated in manufacturing than the German, and much more concentrated in retail and wholesale trade and in services.[3] Coupled with interindustry differences in technology, the countries' different distributions of employment may together generate differences in the timing of work and in the relationships among various temporal aggregates of work time.

This large array of institutional and other differences requires constant attention in the subsequent analyses so that we can be sure that any international differences in the outcomes that we examine do not merely result from the different ways in which the countries' economies and societies are structured. Obversely, the existence of these differences means that outcomes that are uniform across the two countries might be viewed as being fairly typical of the labor markets in industrialized countries more generally.

Table 1.2   Industrial Distribution of Employment, United States, 1991, and Germany, 1990 (Percent of Nonagricultural Employment)

Industry	United States	Germany
Mining (Energy and mining in Germany)	0.6	1.7
Construction	4.3	7.0
Manufacturing	16.9	32.5
Trade	23.3	13.6
Transport and public utilities	5.3	5.8
Finance, insurance and real estate	6.2	3.2
Services	26.4	16.0
Government	17.0	15.6
Private household, including nonprofits		4.6

SOURCE: *Economic Report of the President*, 1992; Institut für Arbeitsmarkt und Berufsforschung, *Zahlen-Fibel*, 1992.

In any study that considers labor market outcomes of any sort, one must be very hesitant in drawing conclusions about the results' importance for policy and their implications for changes in policy. Indeed, whether policies in a particular area are even necessary, much less how they might be structured, is a consideration that should induce more than a touch of modesty in the researcher/author. That is even more true in a study that examines outcomes in two countries, since even similar outcomes and apparently similar institutions do not necessarily imply that the same policy will be equally effective, or even have an effect in the same direction, if applied in both countries (Hamermesh 1995). For these reasons the discussion of policies in this monograph is in most instances at a fairly general level. Nonetheless, the results of the analyses are sufficiently relevant for a variety of types of policies that readers can draw their own conclusions about what specific measures they might imply.

An Overview of the Data

For over 20 years the United States Bureau of Labor Statistics (BLS) has included information on multiple job-holding as part of the May Current Population Survey. From 1973-78, in 1985, and again in 1991 questions about the timing of work were added to the regular Multiple Jobholding Supplement to the May survey. These elicited information on the number of days per week and hours per day (or per week) on each job, and when each job typically began and finished. In this monograph I base much of the empirical research for the United States on the May 1991 Supplement and related data. These data are used by themselves in chapter 3 and also linked to the March 1991 CPS in chapter 2 to examine the relation of days and hours to weeks worked. The May 1977 and 1978 Supplements are combined to form a panel of data on individual workers and are used in the analyses in chapter 4, since they provide the most recent available information on a sample of workers whose timing of work is observed in two years. The May 1985 and May 1991 Supplements are used in chapter 5, along with information from the national income and product accounts. No other set of American data provides information on both days and daily hours, and on the timing of work. No other set of data provides a large random sample of the entire American workforce.

No comparably large publicly available German survey has the same information as the May CPS Supplements. Similar data are available, however, from the German Socioeconomic Panel (hereafter GSOEP), an ongoing study of roughly 9,000 people in the former West Germany that began in 1984 and to which a panel of approximately 5,000 East Germans was added in 1990. This set of data has already received substantial attention from both German and American researchers. (Gerlach and Hübler 1992 and Hunt 1995 are two of many examples.) Information about the number of days per week and hours per day on the main job was obtained in the seventh (1990) wave. The survey also elicited information on some aspects of the timing of work, particularly work in the evenings, at night, and on weekends. Unlike the CPS, this wave of the GSOEP also has potentially useful information on workers' attitudes and problems in scheduling work. The 1990 wave of the GSOEP provides most of the data for this study. In the

1992 wave, members of the sample were also reinterviewed about their days and daily hours of work, and these data are combined with the same information for 1990 to provide the longitudinal information that is used in the analyses in chapter 4.

In an attempt to make the results for the two countries as closely comparable as possible, in each part of each chapter where data from both countries are used I present each table in two forms, one labeled (U) for the United States, the other labeled (G) for the Federal Republic of Germany. While the underlying data are never identical, I aggregate up the data set offering more detail where the sacrifice in information is not too great (usually, the American CPS data) to facilitate cross-country comparisons.

Outline of the Monograph

The second chapter of this monograph examines the determinants of days per week and daily hours of work in the two countries, as well as how these differ depending on workers' differing attachment to the labor force. The major focus here is how these alternative dimensions of work time are correlated with various measures of demographic and socioeconomic status. The chapter also explores how important work schedules are that differ from the eight-hour day and five-day week that we have come to believe is standard.

Chapter 3 studies the instantaneous use of time as it is divided between work and nonwork activities. Much of the focus in the chapter is on establishing some simple facts about the patterns of timing of work and how they vary across labor force participants. Additional analysis centers on how decision making within marriage affects spouses' timing of work.

The analyses in chapters 2 and 3 are based on cross-section data. Chapter 4 uses the 1977–78 panel data constructed for this project and departs from that mode of research to examine how decisions about days and daily hours, and about the timing of work, respond to changes in individuals' circumstances. Of interest here is the effect of changing jobs on work schedules and patterns, particularly whether days or daily hours are altered more and how different kinds of workers change them differently when they switch jobs.

Chapter 5 analyzes how employers combine workers, daily hours, and days per week in production. The focus here, unlike the other chapters, is on labor demand; and unlike those chapters, I present little comparative analysis. The results of the chapter are directly relevant for considering how one might alter public policy to provide incentives for a shorter workweek with as little disruption as possible to production.

The end result of the large amount of evidence presented should, I hope, be to make it clear that we can expand our knowledge of people's labor supply and other aspects of their use of time by moving beyond the very stale concepts of weekly hours and weeks worked. Increasing numbers of sets of data now provide information on days worked per week and daily hours, so that restricting analyses to their product, weekly hours, is no longer necessary. More important, we are beginning to have information on when people work (and not merely on whether they work according to such concepts as "evening shifts" or "night shifts"), so that we can use the notion of instantaneous time use to study people's individual and joint demands for leisure. Chapter 6 outlines the new knowledge that the approach here has made possible in terms of understanding how labor markets work, comparing labor markets in two major countries, and devising labor market policies.

NOTES

1. For example, the Time Use Study of the University of Michigan collected diaries covering each quarter-hour of time for four days in a year. These are instantaneous data; but well-known studies integrate them (Stafford and Duncan 1980; Biddle and Hamermesh 1990), and I am unaware of any research that uses their instantaneous characteristics. The same uniformity—integrating data that have been collected on an instantaneous basis—characterizes the international comparisons of time use in Szalai (1972).

2. *Wall Street Journal*, July 14, 1994, p. B1.

3. An alternative comparison (Appelbaum and Schettkat 1990) that also used the CPS but was based on the German *Mikrozensus* shows for 1987 that 25 percent of U.S. employment was in construction and manufacturing, compared to 41 percent in Germany.

CHAPTER 2

Patterns of Workdays and Hours

In this chapter I analyze days and daily hours of work by individuals in the United States and Germany. The focus is mainly on demographic differences in these dimensions of time use. The standard approach to workers' use of time in the labor market has been to examine the supply of workhours per week. This approach has underlain huge amounts of research and has been made possible because labor force surveys concentrate on the question, "How many hours did you work during the previous week?"

One very straightforward issue is whether the standard approach ignores important aspects of behavior. We can write weekly hours of work as hours per day times days per week. But are the determinants of hours and days the same? Do hours and days respond the same way to the factors that cause them to vary? If the answer to either of these questions is no, then by ignoring the distinction between days and daily hours of work, past research would have failed to provide as complete information as is possible about the determinants of work time. The issue is whether alternative integrations of time use can add to our understanding of the labor market.

This potential problem in our understanding of labor supply is important for a variety of reasons. The possibilities for restructuring work can be informed by studying novel integrations of time use. We are unlikely to learn much about workers' interest in going on four-day weeks based on the typical studies of weekly workhours, even when these are supplemented by the analysis of annual weeks of work. Examining novel disaggregations of integrated time use can also be helpful in studying the demand for child care. Part of the costs of child care are fixed; but fixed over what integration of time: days, weeks, months, or years? Surely at least some fixities must arise each day, so that studying weekly or annual workhours will miss at least some of them.

This chapter first examines how one should analyze alternative integrations of time use, why those alternatives might be interesting, and what are the implications of the theory of labor supply for patterns of days and daily hours. It then discusses the information that the CPS and the GSOEP provide on these concepts, presents some preliminary results on patterns in them, and examines how workdays and daily hours vary together. The rest of the chapter is then devoted to analyzing the determinants of these two aspects of time use.

Analyzing Alternative Integrations of Time Use

The labor market outcomes that we observe—weeks of work, weekly hours, workdays, and daily hours—result from the behavior of a huge array of agents, including businesses, workers, and governments. The process that determines these outcomes is even more complex than simple interactions among these agents would suggest, because the actions of some firms and workers may make it advantageous for others to schedule their activities differently from what would be their choice *in vacuo* (Weiss 1996). For example, choices made by judges and attorneys about the timing of courtroom activities determine much of the work schedule of the independent contractors who serve as court reporters. These considerations suggest that a general approach to analyzing alternative integrations of time use would require a complete model embodying both demand and supply behavior and accounting for externalities in scheduling.

No such general approach has ever been presented even for the standard integration of time use into hours per week. Indeed, even a partial approach that ignores the externalities but considers the behavior of firms and workers simultaneously has not been used to analyze the extremely fruitful microeconomic labor force data that are available in most countries. Instead, the study of integral time use has rested mainly on the empirical implementation of the theory of labor supply. The analysis in this chapter is no different in foregoing the construction of such a general model and basing the discussion mostly on the theory of labor supply. The discussion does, however, recognize that the outcomes (the demographic differences that we observe) can result from both demand and supply forces. For that reason I do not delve deeply into their implications for the structure of workers' preferences and firms' technologies, but instead limit the conclusions mainly to inferences about the determinants of and correlates with the novel integration of time use that this chapter examines.

The problem in any particular aggregation of work time is to determine what the fixed costs are and what are the marginal costs of an extra unit along that dimension. From the supply side, the fixed costs of working at all—the fixed costs of labor force participation—are those associated with making oneself minimally presentable for work. Thus, for example, attorneys or salespeople must be decently groomed whether they are working two hours on one day per week or ten hours on six days each week. These are the standard fixed costs that have been analyzed in the literature on labor supply.

For our purposes those particular fixed costs are not important. What is important is that each worker also faces the fixed costs of adding another day to the workweek, regardless of how many hours are worked on that day. Commuting time is a fixed cost of adding a day of work, since it remains the same whether one stays at the workplace two or ten hours each day. For single parents or two-earner households, some arrangement about child care must be made whether the child is left for one hour or many, implying that there is some fixed daily cost (at least in terms of parents' time) to child care. The main point is that the fixed costs of work occur along several dimensions. At least in theory they are broader than just those costs that are incurred when the worker decides to enter the labor force.

The typical employer may also face differences in the cost of an hour of work or a day of work. In chapter 5, where the analysis is based on aggregates of data that might be viewed as representing firms, I examine some of these costs more closely. To the extent that they are large they too will affect the patterns of workdays and workhours that we observe in the labor force. Were the proper data available—in particular, detailed information on these costs on both the supply and demand sides of the labor market—it would be appropriate to construct a model that explicitly incorporates the relative prices of each dimension of work time. Without such data the best we can accomplish is to use the notions of differences in fixed costs to motivate the interpretation of the outcomes we observe. Whether these notions are important is in the end an empirical question that this chapter will resolve.

The analysis of labor supply under alternative integrations of time is well worked out by Hanoch (1980a) and hardly merits much discussion here. Regardless of the integration that is used, a rise in the price of time (the wage rate) induces the usual possible increases and decreases in labor supply through the substitution and income effects. The existence of fixed costs along a particular dimension, however, can produce the unusual result of large jumps in labor supply along that dimension when the worker's wage rate changes.

Relying on the role of fixed costs in producing these jumps, a potentially useful way of gauging the relative importance of those costs along different dimensions is to examine the relative variability of outcomes along them among otherwise identical individuals. If everyone works a five-day week, but daily hours vary greatly among workers, we may infer that the major source of fixed costs results from the daily costs of working, not from labor force participation *per se*. If the outcomes are about equally variable, we may conclude that there is nothing special about days of work, but rather that the fixed costs of working arise from labor force participation itself. If that is the case, we may infer that there is little new to be learned from further research that distinguishes between days and daily hours, and that the usual data on weekly hours of work and employment status provide sufficient information from which to infer the behavior of labor supply.

Most researchers in the voluminous and by now extremely technical literature on labor supply have ignored the issue of fixed costs altogether, concentrating only on one dimension of labor supply (usually participation or weekly hours) or analyzing two dimensions (usually these two together) but ignoring problems of fixed costs. A small number of studies have examined the size of the fixed costs of participating in the labor force in the context of a model of hours of work. Cogan (1980) studied how fixed costs of participation affect annual work hours. Hanoch (1980b), Blank (1988) and Triest (1990) have all examined three dimensions of labor supply—participation, weekly hours (in a survey week), and weeks worked (in the previous year)—in the context of models in which fixed costs arise on different dimensions of time use. By inference this literature demonstrates that it is inappropriate to aggregate weekly hours and annual weeks into annual hours of work, since the estimates suggest that demographic and other factors have different effects along these dimensions. The results show that there is something to be learned from classifying total hours of work along different dimensions.

There has been essentially no empirical study of the distinction between days per week and hours per day, whether it be simply analyzing their correlation, discovering their determinants, or placing them in a complete model of labor supply with alternative types of fixed costs. Aside from the potential attraction of this distinction because of the light it might shed on various areas of policy interest, it can also thus provide a clearer test of whether it is important to use a finer temporal aggregation than the standard measure, weekly hours of work. Finding differences in the importance of various correlates of days and weeks would provide additional and perhaps stronger evidence of the inappropriately high level of aggregation over time that we usually use in analyzing labor market outcomes involving time use.

Studying the integration of time use into workdays and daily hours has an additional advantage over some other integrations. The data used to analyze weekly hours are recorded as the worker's response to questions about last week's activities, so that the many studies that concentrate on this one dimension of time use are based on data that are likely to be fairly free of errors induced because people cannot remember what they have been doing with their time. When researchers have gone beyond this, e.g., to measure both weekly hours and annual workweeks, they have relied on people's responses at a point in time (for example, March 1996) about a relatively large part of their work histories (for example, their activities during all of 1995). Such studies are thus based on data characterized by potential errors resulting from workers' difficulties in recalling their activities over the previous year. No such problem exists in the particular integration of work time into workdays and hours per day, since information about both dimensions is based on workers' responses about their current labor market activities.

Measuring Days and Daily Hours

To make it very clear exactly what we are discussing, I detail the questions to which interviewees in the CPS and GSOEP responded.

The May 1991 CPS Multiple Jobholding Supplement asked people who held at least one job, "How many days a week [do you] usually work at this job?" This is the variable that I use to measure DAYS. The possible answers include 1, 2, up through 7, as well as 4-1/2 or 5-1/2 days as separate responses (that I include with 5 and 6 days, respectively, in the simple tabulations that follow). The survey also asks, "How many hours per day [do you] usually work at this job?", which measures HOURS and can range from 1 upward. For comparative purposes I also examine actual weekly hours, the standard CPS measure of time worked, which presumably includes hours on all jobs.

For one-half the May 1991 CPS sample (rotation groups 3, 4, 7 and 8) it is possible to link the March and May 1991 CPS samples to obtain information on part- and full-time weeks worked in 1990 (available only in the March CPS). This permits examining whether current DAYS and HOURS have the same relation to longer-term attachment to the labor force. Finally, all the usual demographic information from the CPS is available (such as education, age, family structure, and children by age) and is used to study whether the correlates of DAYS and HOURS are the same.

The analogous questions in the 1990 wave of the GSOEP generate DAYS as the integer response to the question, "How many days per week do you usually work?" and HOURS as the response to, "How many hours do you usually work per day?" Actual weekly hours are responses to, "On average, how much is your actual work time [per week], including any overtime?"[1] The concepts of usual DAYS and usual HOURS per day are measured as similarly to the CPS as is possible given inherent differences in culture and language. Actual weekly hours may not be measured quite so similarly in the GSOEP, since the GSOEP explicitly mentions overtime in asking about actual hours and asks this question in the context of a set of questions about the main job.

Respondents in the GSOEP were also asked to check off for each month in 1989 whether they worked full time, part time, or not at all. While this is a different integration of time from the measure of the previous year's weeks of work in the CPS, these responses do at least offer evidence on the same part time/full time distinction available from the CPS. Finally, like most smaller panels of household data the GSOEP offers much more demographic information than the CPS, so that we have more than enough information to analyze the same correlates of workdays and daily hours as for the United States.

While information on DAYS and HOURS is available in the CPS for workers whose schedules are irregular, it is not present in the GSOEP. Because of this and the desire to maintain comparability between the results for the United States and Germany, all the analysis in this chapter is based on workers who are on regular schedules on their main jobs. A more general issue is whether the hours measures represent time actually worked or time paid for (including sick time, vacations, etc.) Since the measures of DAYS and HOURS are self-reported by the workers in the households sampled by the CPS and the GSOEP, there is no sure way of answering this question. What is clear, however, is that their responses refer to a typical week of work, and as such should be interpreted as reflecting their average effort on the job over a longer period of time. Moreover, since the underlying questions are essentially identical in the two surveys, we can be fairly certain that cross-country comparisons in this chapter are not contaminated by any basic differences in how the concepts are measured.

Questions about work on second jobs were asked in the CPS and the GSOEP, but they are not completely comparable to those asked about the primary job and are, in any case, only available for one-third of dual job holders. The CPS gives days per week on second jobs, but it only asks about total hours per week, not daily hours on those jobs. The GSOEP asks about daily hours on any second job, but only obtains information on days worked per month on them. These differences in the information elicited about first and second jobs, especially the absence from the GSOEP of information on which days the person works the second job, make it impossible to construct a measure of total days that each labor force participant is at work in each country and the total hours worked on the typical day. That data problem alone rationalizes restricting the analysis in this chapter to information about days and daily hours on the main job. I thus present evidence on integrated time use on a job and not precisely on the integration of time use over all 168 hours available to each person during the week.

How important is this neglect of days and hours on second jobs? Table 2.1 shows the distribution of hours per week on second jobs in the two countries in these surveys. As noted in chapter 1, moonlighting is fairly uncommon in both countries. Moreover, especially in Germany those few workers who hold second jobs usually work at the second job very few hours per week. Moreover, only half of the 6.6 percent of American workers who moonlight work on their second job more than two days per week. Among the 7.2 percent of German workers who report a second job, only half report working at that job more than one day per week (in the questionnaire, more than four days per month), and only half report working at the second job more than three hours on average on the days they work at their second job. That being the case, we may infer that except for the very few workers who hold long second jobs (less than 2 percent of the U.S. workforce, almost no German workers), our measure of daily hours is correct for the typical workday. Any biases or errors in the results in this chapter because of the lack of information about daily hours and days on second jobs are likely to be very minor indeed.

Table 2.1   Percent Distributions of Workers by Usual Hours on Second Job, United States, 1991, Germany, 1990

Usual hours on second job	United States	Germany
0	93.4	92.8
1–9	2.7	5.8
10–14	1.1	0.9
15–19	0.9	0.2
>19	1.9	0.3

Tables 2.2U and 2.2G present for the two countries the distributions of workers by the regularity of their schedules. The concepts of regularity differ in the two surveys, but I assume that a rotating shift in Germany would be included as one of the three types of irregular schedules reported in the CPS. Thus the best comparison is between the percentages of workers whose schedules, or days and hours, are regular.

The similarity in the regularity of scheduled days and hours between the two countries is remarkable. Roughly seven-eighths of workers in both countries have fixed schedules on their main jobs (at least using the time integrations days per week and hours per day). Given the substantial differences in the industrial structures of the German and U.S. labor forces that were shown in table 1.2, this similarity is all the more surprising. There is also little difference by gender in the extent of fix-ity of days/hours schedules among employed workers. This too is somewhat surprising, given the well-known differences by gender in weekly hours, labor force attachment, and the distribution of workers by industry.

Table 2.2U   Percent Distributions of Workers by Type of Work Schedule, Main Job, 1991

	All workers	Male	Female
Regular schedules	86.1	85.7	86.6
Rotating or split-shifts	4.3	4.7	3.8
Irregular or other	9.6	9.6	9.5
Number of observations:			
N =	61501	32853	28648

Table 2.2G   Percent Distributions of Workers by Type of Work Schedule, Main Job, 1990

	All workers	Male	Female
Regular days and hours	87.5	87.4	87.5
Regular days, irregular hours	6.6	7.0	6.0
Regular hours, irregular days	3.4	3.1	3.8
Irregular hours and days	2.5	2.4	2.6
Number of observations:			
N =	5176	3122	2054

The estimates in tables 2.2 are presented for all civilian workers. But excluding those who have a second job, or those currently enrolled in school, does not change the results. In the United States, excluding school enrollees raises the percentage of workers who are on regular schedules to 87.0, while excluding the 6.6 percent of workers with any second job (even a very short one) raises the percent of workers on such schedules just barely (to 86.2). In table 2.2G the first percentage drops to 87.2, while the second rises minutely to 87.6. It is interesting to note that these results show that workers who are in school in the United States are much more likely to work irregular schedules than those who are not in school. In Germany, differences in schedules between school enrollees and others are less pronounced, again evidence for the greater uniformity of schedules there than in the United States.

Patterns of Days, Daily Hours and Workweeks

While I examine the determinants of DAYS and HOURS later in this chapter, we can learn much about patterns of working time just by considering cross-tabulations of these two aggregates of time use. Several authors have presented distributions of days per week and daily hours separately (Brown et al. 1986 for the United Kingdom, and Bell and Freeman 1995 for the United States and Germany), but only Hamermesh (1995) presented distributions of days and hours jointly, and his information for the United States was based on a very small and also outdated sample.

Tables 2.3 present these cross-tabulations for the United States and Germany. Patterns of daily hours, independent of days worked, do not differ greatly between the countries, especially when we remember that the German workday was shortened in the late 1980s for many people and consider the entire range of 7.0 to 8.0 hours per day inclusive. There is less weight in the distribution in the United States in the range from 8.1 to 9.9 hours inclusive, but much more weight at the upper tail of this distribution. More people in the United States than in Germany work very long hours. The evidence in table 2.1 implies that, were this comparison to include work on second jobs, the cross-country differences would be slightly larger.

The bigger international difference is in the distribution of workdays. Jobs in the United States are much less standardized on a five-day workweek than jobs in Germany: Only three-fourths of American workers put in five days per week on their main jobs, while nearly seven-eighths of German workers do. Implicitly it is much easier to tailor work schedules to workers' preferences or employers' demands in the United States. Additional tabulations show that this difference holds true even if we exclude manufacturing workers (who form, as table 1.2 showed, a substantially greater fraction of the workforce in

Table 2.3U Distribution of Hours per Day and Days per Week, Main Job, 1991 (Percent Distributions)

HOURS PER DAY	DAYS PER WEEK			
	1–4	5	6–7	All days
	Employees (N = 56493)			
≤4.0	2.7	3.1	.6	6.4
4.0–6.9	3.0	3.9	1.1	8.1
7.0–7.9	1.0	4.0	.6	5.6
8.0	3.7	50.9	3.1	57.7
8.1–9.9	.4	5.4	1.8	7.6
≥10	2.9	6.7	4.9	14.6
All hours	13.7	74.0	12.3	
	Self-employed (N = 5290)			
≤4.0	4.9	4.0	2.2	11.1
4.0–6.9	3.5	4.5	4.0	12.0
7.0–7.9	.8	2.4	2.0	5.2
8.0	2.7	18.5	7.6	28.8
8.1–9.9	.4	3.6	5.1	9.2
≥10	1.7	8.8	23.1	33.7
All hours	14.0	42.0	44.0	
	Male employees (N = 29452)			
≤4.0	1.6	1.8	.6	4.0
4.0–6.9	1.8	2.2	1.0	4.9
7.0–7.9	.4	2.1	.6	3.1
8.0	2.0	51.8	4.2	58.0
8.1–9.9	.2	6.5	2.6	9.3
≥10	3.3	9.5	7.8	20.6
All hours	9.3	73.8	16.8	
	Female employees (N = 27041)			
≤4.0	3.9	4.5	.7	9.1
4.0–6.9	4.4	5.8	1.3	11.6
7.0–7.9	1.6	6.0	.7	8.2
8.0	5.6	49.9	1.9	57.4
8.1–9.9	.5	4.2	1.0	5.7
≥10	2.5	3.6	1.8	7.9
All hours	18.6	74.1	7.3	

NOTE: Totals do not add to 100 percent because of rounding.

Table 2.3G Distribution of Hours per Day and Days per Week, Main Job, 1990 (Percent Distributions)

HOURS PER DAY	DAYS PER WEEK			
	1–4	5	6–7	All days
	Employees (N = 4333)			
≤4.0	1.1	4.8	.7	6.6
4.0–6.9	.9	3.9	1.6	6.5
7.0–7.9	.5	19.0	1.3	20.8
8.0	1.0	39.6	2.7	43.3
8.1–9.9	.4	14.4	1.3	16.6
≥10	.4	4.6	1.8	6.8
All hours	4.2	86.3	9.5	
	Self-employed (N = 194)			
≤4.0	6.2	1.0	0	7.2
4.0–6.9	1.6	2.6	1.6	5.7
7.0–7.9	.5	1.0	2.1	3.6
8.0	1.0	7.2	5.7	13.9
8.1–9.9	0	5.1	9.8	15.0
≥10	.5	9.8	44.3	54.6
All hours	9.8	26.8	63.4	
	Male employees (N = 2603)			
≤4.0	.3	.4	.1	.7
4.0–6.9	.3	.5	.7	1.5
7.0–7.9	.4	20.8	1.2	22.4
8.0	.4	44.2	2.9	47.5
8.1–9.9	.1	17.2	1.6	18.9
≥10	.2	6.4	2.4	9.0
All hours	1.7	89.4	8.9	
	Female employees (N = 1730)			
≤4.0	2.4	11.5	1.7	15.6
4.0–6.9	1.9	9.1	3.0	14.0
7.0–7.9	.7	16.2	1.4	18.3
8.0	1.8	32.8	2.4	37.1
8.1–9.9	.7	10.2	.8	11.7
≥10	.6	1.9	.9	3.4
All hours	8.1	81.7	10.2	

NOTE: Totals do not add to 100 percent because of rounding.

Germany than in the United States). The cross-country difference is not merely a matter of technology and industrial structure, but may instead reflect a combination of institutional differences and workers' preferences for schedules. The outcome may be a reason for the often-cited flexibility of the U.S. labor market vis-à-vis those in the European Union (e.g., Abraham and Houseman 1993) in response to cost and demand shocks that necessitate restructuring of the workforce.

The eight-hour day in a five-day week is widely prevalent in both countries. When we use the range 7.0 to 8.0 hours per day inclusive, we see that 55 percent of U.S. employees and 59 percent of German employees work a standard week in terms of both days and hours per day. Nonetheless, a surprisingly large number of workers have primary jobs with unusually long (>8) hours on few (<5) days: 3.3 percent of employees in the United States and 0.8 percent in Germany. Obversely, substantial numbers of workers have jobs with short (<7) daily hours spread over many (>5) days per week: 1.7 percent of U.S. employees and 2.3 percent of German employees work on these schedules. Clearly, long workdays do not uniformly imply long workweeks. Substantial numbers of workers have unbalanced schedules in the sense that days of work are many and daily hours are few, or vice-versa.

Over 50 percent of both men and women work standard schedules of hours per day and days per week in the United States; and the percentages working 5 days per week or 8 hours per day are also the same by gender. In Germany (where female participation rates are lower than in the United States) many fewer women than men work the normal workweek of 5 days and 7-8 hours; and fewer women are working 5 days or 7-8 hours per day on any schedule. More American women than men work few days per week, and fewer women work 6 or 7 days. Similarly, more women work short days, and fewer women work more than 8 hours. These differences by gender are only partly mirrored in the German workforce. That nearly one-third of female workers in Germany have short working days, and that many more women than men work few days per week, contribute to women's shorter workweeks in Germany than in the United States. The short working days may arise from work by women with children whose school days limit their mothers' working hours (in a country where classes are usually only in the morning). Despite, or perhaps because of the high fraction of German women who work short daily hours, a large fraction of German women workers are at work on more than five days per week. This fraction exceeds that among German men and among American women.

Tables 2.3 also demonstrate the importance of distinguishing between employees and the self-employed (who presumably have more control over the days and daily hours they work). In both countries there is much less standardization of both days and hours among self-employed workers. Many more self-employed workers have long daily schedules and work many days; but many more also work few daily hours and/or few days per week. One well-known difference between employees and the self-employed in the United States is that the variance in annual earnings within a group of self-employed workers is greater than within a group of employees. This may be due to the fact the variance in the hourly wage rates among self-employed workers is greater than that among employees. The evidence here, however, suggests that it is also at least partly a result of the greater variance and skewness in *both* their workdays and daily hours worked.[2] The differences in work schedules between these two types of worker are essentially the same in both countries, even though the schedules of some German self-employed workers (shop-owners and independent craft workers) are constrained by very stringent laws regulating shopping hours.[3]

That the information about workers' daily hours tells us relatively little about their days worked per week is supported by the very low pairwise correlations (shown in tables 2.4) between DAYS and HOURS. Among employees, long daily hours do not imply many days of work; the obverse is also true. The same low correlations are observed even if we exclude students from the samples on which the correlations in tables 2.4 are based. While the low correlation exists among employees, the self-employed in both Germany and the United States who choose to work long hours also choose to work many days per week.

Despite this demonstration that DAYS and HOURS do not covary greatly among employees, tables 2.4 show that both covary strongly with actual weekly hours. The general inference is the unsurprising one that differences in both temporal aggregates of work time contribute to differences in the length of the actual workweek. The correlation is

Table 2.4U   Correlations of Dimensions of Work Time, Workers with One Job in 1991

| | Employees (N=22477) | | | |
	Days per week	Hours per day	Actual weekly hours	Weeks full time, 1990
Hours per day	0.20			
Actual weekly hours	0.56	0.66		
Weeks full time, 1990	0.39	0.42	0.51	
Weeks total, 1990	0.18	0.20	0.24	0.56
	Self-employed (N=2224)			
	Days per week	Hours per day	Actual weekly hours	Weeks full time, 1990
Hours per day	0.37			
Actual weekly hours	0.62	0.71		
Weeks full time, 1990	0.43	0.46	0.51	
Weeks total, 1990	0.24	0.18	0.24	0.51
	Male employees (N=11857)			
	Days per week	Hours per day	Actual weekly hours	Weeks full time, 1990
Hours per day	0.15			
Actual weekly hours	0.51	0.63		
Weeks full time, 1990	0.29	0.33	0.40	
Weeks total, 1990	0.14	0.17	0.20	0.64
	Female employees (N=10620)			
	Days per week	Hours per day	Actual weekly hours	Weeks full time, 1990
Hours per day	0.19			
Actual weekly hours	0.59	0.64		
Weeks full time, 1990	0.42	0.45	0.58	
Weeks total, 1990	0.19	0.20	0.26	0.50

Table 2.4G   Correlations of Dimensions of Work Time, Main Job, Workers with Regular Schedules, 1990

	Days per week	Hours per day	Actual weekly hours	Months full time, 1990
	Employees (N=4333)			
Hours per day	0.13			
Actual weekly hours	0.43	0.72		
Months full time, 1989	0.23	0.50	0.52	
Months total, 1989	0.08	0.05	0.08	0.66
	Self-employed (N=194)			
Hours per day	0.61			
Actual weekly hours	0.68	0.75		
Months full time, 1989	0.59	0.58	0.58	
Months total, 1989	0.09	0.14	0.12	0.42
	Male employees (N=2603)			
Hours per day	0.13			
Actual weekly hours	0.42	0.58		
Months full time, 1989	0.20	0.12	0.20	
Months total, 1989	0.10	0.07	0.13	0.95
	Female employees (N=1730)			
Hours per day	0.08			
Actual weekly hours	0.42	0.75		
Months full time, 1989	0.22	0.60	0.61	
Months total, 1989	0.05	0.00	−0.01	0.47

much higher with HOURS than with DAYS in Germany, but only slightly higher in the United States. Nonetheless, in both countries the more important determinant of a worker's weekly hours is his or her daily hours, not the days worked per week. Moreover, other classifications of days and hours (to account for the discreteness of the choices) provide the same conclusion. The result underlines the major general finding of this chapter, namely, that rigidities in working schedules appear to be those involved in changing the number of days worked more than in changing daily hours.[4]

Among men the correlations of DAYS and HOURS with the full-time weeks (months in Germany) worked by these current labor force participants in the previous year are of little interest, since much of the variation in weeks (months) in these samples measures unemployment rather than nonparticipation. Among women the correlations of weeks worked (months worked in Germany) with HOURS are quite high: women who work more hours per day worked more weeks during the previous year. Especially in Germany, but to a lesser extent in the United States too, the correlation of recent full-time work with current days per week is lower than with daily hours.

The Determinants of Time Use Along Three Dimensions

Research by economists and other social scientists has established clearly the correlates of weekly hours. We know that there is a life cycle in weekly and annual hours of work, and that women's labor supply is negatively related to their household responsibilities, particularly to the presence of young children. Whether these correlations arise from a relationship of the correlates with days of work, daily hours, or both, and if both correlations exist whether they are the same size, is unknown and is the subject of this section.

I present estimates of equations describing the logarithms of days and daily hours. It is worth noting again that these do not describe separately the structure of workers' and employers' behavior, but are instead the reduced-form result of the interaction of behavior by both households and firms. The covariates included in the equations are age and age squared, age of youngest child (the excluded category is youngest child over age 5), marital status, ethnicity/race (in the United States) or foreign-born (in Germany), and years of education. In the United States this is just the highest grade of formal schooling completed, ranging from 0 to 18 years; in Germany, where apprenticeships and other formal on-the-job training substitute for formal schooling for some workers, an algorithm that adds years of formal schooling and years of different types of training is used to generate a measure of total years of schooling.[5]

Also included in the estimates for the United States is the unemployment rate in the metropolitan area.[6] We know that weekly hours are procyclical; but is this relation between hours per week and unemployment due more to the procyclicality of days or of hours per day? The question is important for a variety of reasons, including analyzing possibilities for work-sharing (for example, through offering short-time compensation for reduced days per week), basing partial unemployment benefits on weekly hours or days of work, and analyzing cyclical variations in labor productivity. Using cross-section variation in unemployment is a poor substitute for information on how days and hours vary cyclically, since much of any cross-section difference in unemployment is permanent. But so long as at least some of these differences result partly from interarea differences in the extent of labor market disequilibria, estimating the impact of area unemployment rates on days and daily hours of work may be somewhat informative about cyclical effects.

The estimates are presented in the tables 2.5.[7] It is well known (at least for the American labor force, as Ghez and Becker 1975 show) that there is a life cycle in weekly and annual hours of work: among a group of workers observed at a point in time, weekly and annual hours increase up to some age, then decrease thereafter.[8] But is this inverse U-shaped pattern a result of patterns of days worked or more a result of patterns of daily hours of work over the life cycle? The answer seems quite clear from the estimates. It is true that in the United States and Germany both days and daily hours increase with age up to peaks in the forties and then decline. In both countries and for both genders, however, the inverse U-shaped pattern is steeper for daily hours than for days (though the difference is insignificant for German women). Most of the life-cycle pattern in hours of work is due to a life cycle in daily hours.[9]

Table 2.5U   OLS Estimates of Coefficients in the Determinants of log(Days per Week) and log(Hours per Day), Employees, Main Job, 1991

	Males		Females	
	Days	**Hours**	**Days**	**Hours**
Age	.0205	.0371	.0229	.0347
	(.0005)	(.0007)	(.0008)	(.0009)
$Age^2/100$	−.0241	−.0432	−.0274	−.0403
	(.0006)	(.0008)	(.0009)	(.0010)
Age youngest child:				
<3	.0185	.0343	−.0468	−.0054
	(.0039)	(.0049)	(.0061)	(.0068)
3–5	.0044	.0156	−.0388	−.0350
	(.0045)	(.0056)	(.0066)	(.0073)
Married	.0057	.0358	−.0326	−.0366
	(.0030)	(.0037)	(.0037)	(.0042)
Black	.0007	−.0344	.0370	.0238
	(.0045)	(.0056)	(.0057)	(.0063)
Hispanic	.0237	−.0086	.0527	.0295
	(.0046)	(.0057)	(.0071)	(.0080)
Asian	−.0021	−.0595	.0400	.0006
	(.0069)	(.0085)	(.0100)	(.0111)
Other race	.0082	−.0148	.0333	.0178
	(.0118)	(.0146)	(.0160)	(.0179)
Area unemployment rate	−.0005	−.0013	−.0003	−.0019
	(.0007)	(.0008)	(.0010)	(.0011)
Years of schooling	.0031	.0053	.0011	.0138
	(.0004)	(.0005)	(.0007)	(.0008)
$\overline{R}^2$	.064	.145	.042	.080
N =	29452		27041	

NOTE: Standard errors in parentheses below the estimates.

Table 2.5G   OLS Estimates of Coefficients in the Determinants of log(Days per Week) and log(Hours per Day), Employees, Main Job, 1990

	Males		Females	
	Days	**Hours**	**Days**	**Hours**
Age	.0059	.0099	.0027	−.0031
	(.0015)	(.0023)	(.0033)	(.0055)
Age^2/100	−.0067	−.0122	−.0043	−.0046
	(.0018)	(.0029)	(.0042)	(.0069)
Age youngest child:				
<3	.0073	.0123	−.1649	−.2018
	(.0073)	(.0116)	(.0223)	(.0375)
3–5	.0013	.0180	−.0471	−.1695
	(.0078)	(.0124)	(.0211)	(.0354)
Married or partner	.0020	−.0036	−.0369	−.1364
	(.0066)	(.0105)	(.0135)	(.0227)
Foreign	−.0226	.0190	.0070	−.0371
	(.0101)	(.0160)	(.0235)	(.0395)
Education	−.0002	.0033	−.0005	.0127
	(.0010)	(.0016)	(.0027)	(.0046)
$\bar{R}^2$	.015	.016	.046	.120
N =	2416		1597	

In both the United States and Germany, having young children in the household induces men to work both more days and more daily hours; and in both countries the impacts on daily hours are larger. Consistent with the substantial evidence of their impact on weekly hours, the presence of young children reduces women's days worked in both countries. In the United States, unlike in Germany, the negative effect is mainly on days of work. Since the fixed costs of work are associated with daily commuting and child-care costs, this difference may arise from easier access to child care in Germany (provided in many cases by female relatives who do not participate in the labor force). That the elasticities are generally larger in Germany is consistent with the observation that women's attachment to the labor force is less there than in the United States. Being married without young children induces effects on days and daily hours in the same directions as does having young children in the household. Also, the effects are much larger for German than for American women, suggesting that at least some of the U.S.-German differences have to do with cultural attitudes toward married women working rather than solely with differences in child-care arrangements.

Foreign-born workers in Germany do not work days or hours per day that differ greatly from native workers. Racial/ethnic differences in the United States are also not large, but some are significant and the patterns of differences are very interesting. Even though men's weekly workhours do not differ significantly by race/ethnicity, the evidence in table 2.5U suggests that their composition does. Among both black and Hispanic men, days worked are greater than among non-Hispanic whites, but daily hours are less. The greater rigidity of days than of hours demonstrated earlier in this chapter suggests that the fixed costs are mainly those associated with adding a day of work. That being the case, between any two people with identical weekly earnings and hours of work, the one whose days worked are greater (and whose daily hours are proportionately less) will have lower net weekly earnings after accounting for the fixed daily costs of working. By that interpretation we may conclude that minority/majority differences in hourly or weekly earnings among men understate the extent of differences in net earnings between the groups.

Among black and Hispanic women, both daily hours and workdays significantly exceed those of non-Hispanic white women. We know that the labor force participation of minority females is below that of majority women (although only slightly for black women).[10] Also, however, black women's weekly hours, conditional on their labor force participation, are greater than white women's (Coleman and Pencavel 1993). Racial/ethnic differences are greater for workdays than for daily hours, suggesting for women, as the results also did for men, the existence of racial/ethnic differences in the burdens of the fixed costs of work.

The estimated impacts of area unemployment on days or daily hours shown in table 2.5U are far from being statistically significant. All the coefficients are negative, however, which is consistent with the procyclicality of weekly hours. That the estimated impacts are more negative on daily hours than on days provides a hint that cyclical variation in workhours arises more from variations in the length of the workday than in the number of days worked per week (among those who retain jobs). This suggests that over the business cycle, as is true across individuals, days of work have a larger fixed component than do daily hours.

More educated workers supply more hours to the market each week, as one would expect since education raises the returns to market work. The results for the United States and Germany both show that the impact of education is mainly (in Germany, entirely) through more educated workers putting in longer workdays rather than more days per week. This may be because educated workers have longer (more costly) daily commutes than their less-educated co-workers. Whether or not this is the underlying reason, the results again show that, presumably because of the larger fixed costs of days of work, workers adjust along the (less costly) margin of extra daily hours.

If the approach of this chapter were purely one of workers' freely choosing work schedules based solely on unconstrained choices about combinations of days and hours, there would be no need to go any further in specifying the equations in tables 2.5. In the absence of a formal structural model one should view this chapter just as providing information about the correlates of workdays and daily hours. We can, however, delve a bit further into the issue by making some attempt to account for the costs that employers face in offering different schedules.

There is no information about the particular firms where people in the CPS and GSOEP samples work, and there are no data on the actual costs employers face; but there is information on which industry the worker was employed in. Accordingly, I reestimated all the equations in tables 2.5 including dummy variables for each industry. For the United States these are three-digit industries, while for Germany (for which the sample is much smaller) these are essentially two-digit industries.[11] None of the coefficient estimates changes appreciably when we account for the narrowly defined industry where the individuals work, and none of the conclusions about the correlates of days and hours is changed by allowing for interindustry differences in work schedules. While even this level of detail about industry structure does not remove all demand-side determinants of workdays and daily hours, it surely removes much of them. That the impacts of demographic differences do not change appreciably when we account for differences in industrial structure suggests it is reasonable to infer that those differences result from workers' choices about how to structure their workweeks.

Consider in more detail the behavior of women workers. I want to examine whether their attachment to the labor force, in terms of weeks or months worked in the previous year, varies in the same way as does their choice of weekly schedules. This question is more interesting for women because their attachment to the labor force is on average less than that of men. Tables 2.6 show estimates of equations relating days and weeks of work (months of work in Germany) in the previous year to a variety of correlates among women who worked during the survey week (month in Germany). The samples consist only of women who were working at the time of the survey. The equations are estimated by the ordered-logit technique that accounts for the discrete number of workdays (only 7 possibilities) and workweeks.

The coefficients in the equation describing weeks (months) are generally similar to those in the equation describing days per week. In the estimates describing work during the previous year an interesting, though unsurprising, difference in the United States is the lower weeks of work among minority women, a result that reflects their lower participation rate. Even though married women put in fewer days of market work than single women (and, as tables 2.5 showed, fewer hours too), they have a slightly greater attachment to the labor force than do

34

Table 2.6U   Determinants of Days per Week on Main Job and Weeks per Year, Female Employees with Days>0 in 1991

Variable	Days per week, 1991 (ordered logit)	Weeks worked, 1990[a] (ordered logit)
Age	0.167	0.136
	(0.006)	(0.008)
Age^2/100	−0.197	-0.137
	(0.007)	(0.009)
Age youngest child:		
< 3	-0.306	-0.321
	(0.050)	(0.060)
3-5	-0.272	-0.145
	(0.054)	(0.069)
Married	-0.280	0.046
	(0.031)	(0.041)
Black	0.231	−0.060
	(0.047)	(0.061)
Hispanic	0.439	−0.095
	(0.060)	(0.076)
Asian	0.410	−0.887
	(0.085)	(0.101)
Other race	0.281	−0.740
	(0.136)	(0.160)
Years of schooling	0.010	0.026
	(0.006)	(0.007)
Pseudo-R^2	.017	.024
N =	27041	13509

NOTE: Standard errors in parentheses below estimates.
a. The categories for weeks worked in 1990 are 50-52; 48-49; 40-47; 27-39; 14-26; 1-13, and 0.

Table 2.6G   Determinants of Days per Week on Main Job and Months per Year, Female Employees with Days>0 in 1990

Variable	Days per week (ordered logit)	Months worked, 1989[a] (ordered logit)
Age	-0.064	0.370
	(0.043)	(0.04)
$Age^2/100$	0.078	-0.389
	(0.054)	(0.05)
Age Youngest Child:		
< 3	-1.328	-1.170
	(0.258)	(0.21)
3-5	-0.441	-0.745
	(0.267)	(0.23)
Married or partner	-0.372	0.356
	(0.166)	(0.16)
Foreign born	0.205	-0.390
	(0.291)	(0.28)
Education	–0.0085	0.067
	(0.033)	(0.037)
Pseudo-R^2	.020	.141
N =	1597	

NOTE: Standard errors in parentheses below estimates.

a. The categories for months worked in 1989 are 12; 7-11; 1-6, and 0.

single women who are observed working during a particular week or month. One possible explanation for this difference is that, like married men, married women who choose to work are inherently more stable workers than single women who happen to be working. Clearly, though, this difference is tied to the possibilities for scheduling work and their relation to husbands' work schedules, issues that I deal with in chapter 3.

Conclusions and Implications

By examining some novel temporal aggregates of work time—days per week and hours per day—we have discovered several new facts. Some of these characterize labor markets in both the United States and Germany, while others may highlight how differences in institutional structures and culture generate different labor market outcomes. Among the facts are the following:

There is much greater variation in daily hours than in days worked per week.

Correlations between daily hours and days worked are quite low among employees, but are large and positive among self-employed workers.

Many demographic factors affect daily hours differently from how they affect workdays. Particularly important is the finding that the rise and eventual fall of workhours as people age is due more to changes in daily hours than to changes in days per week.

There is some weak evidence that variations in unemployment affect daily hours more than days per week.

The relative flexibility of the American labor market compared to one European labor market, that of Germany, is manifested chiefly in a greater dispersion of days worked, not daily hours.

Young children reduce married women's supply of days more than they reduce their supply of daily hours in the United States. The opposite is true in Germany (where female labor force participation is lower).

The most general implication of these results is that we cannot treat weekly hours of work as a homogeneous unit. All previous analyses of time use would treat a five-day, eight-hour-per-day workweek identically to a four-day, ten-hour-per-day workweek. The evidence here suggests that they are not identical in terms of the costs that they generate for workers and employers. Implicitly the costs of altering work schedules are associated more with changing the number of days of work than with changing daily hours.

That young children have a bigger negative impact on American mothers' supply of days than of daily hours suggests that the major problem in the availability of child care is the difficulty in overcoming the daily fixed costs of work. The results imply that a subsidy per hour of child care is likely to be less cost-effective in facilitating market work by mothers with young children than one that offers a fixed amount per day of child-care costs incurred.

NOTES

1. "Wie viele Stunden arbeiten Sie in der Regel pro Arbeitstag?" "Wieviel Tage in der Woche arbeiten Sie in der Regel?" and "...wieviel beträgt im Durchschnitt Ihre tatsächliche Arbeitszeit einschliesslich eventueller Überstunden?"

2. For example, data from the 1980 U.S. *Census of Population* show that the mean earnings of white male employees exceeded their median earnings by 10 percent; among white male self-employed workers the excess was 35 percent. A similarly greater skewness appears to exist among German women, though not among German men (OECD 1992, p. 164).

3. The differences between the distributions of hours and days in the two countries do not stem from our inclusion of all workers with regular schedules. Excluding workers with two jobs from these tables makes essentially no difference: In the United States (Germany) the percentage of employees with five-day schedules is 74.2 (86.3), essentially the same as those in the tables. Of workers with only one job, 64.3 (64.5) percent work betwen 7 and 8 hours inclusive, also almost the same as in the tables. Excluding workers who are also students has no effect on the distributions for Germany, but does raise the percentages of American workers on five-day schedules or at work between 7 and 8 hours per day. American students are disproportionately part-day and part-week workers.

4. This inference from the differences in the correlations of DAYS and HOURS with actual weekly hours also shows up in a decomposition of the variance of actual hours into its components.

5. Ken Couch of Syracuse University provided this algorithm to me. It allows years of education to range between 0 and 19, very much like the 0 to 18 years available in the May 1991 CPS.

6. For people resident in a metropolitan area (MSA) this is the average unemployment rate in the area. Workers not located in an MSA are assigned the statewide average unemployment rate.

7. The disturbances in these pairs of equations are positively correlated, but the correlations are quite low (0.13, 0.18, 0.14, and 0.02). Most of the variance in days is truly random, independent of the randomness in hours, and vice-versa.

8. While this is true in a cross-section of individuals, the relationship with age is weaker, but still apparent, if we follow a cohort of workers over their lives (Owen 1986, table 2.7). For our purposes of comparing patterns of days and daily hours with the well-known cross-section patterns of weekly hours the comparison in the text is the relevant one.

9. One might worry that using least-squares regressions based on logarithms of workdays, which are so heavily concentrated at one value (5), may produce errors in the results. Least-

squares is used here for comparison with the appropriate least-squares regressions of daily hours. An examination of the coefficients and the "cut-points" for the ordered logits on workdays in tables 2.6 shows that least-squares analysis does not produce incorrect inferences about the directions or relative magnitudes of the effects of the independent variables.

10. In 1994 the rates for women age 16 or over were 58.9, 58.7, and 52.9 among whites, blacks, and Hispanics, respectively (*Employment and Earnings* January 1995).

11. In the estimates based on the CPS this results in the inclusion of separate constant terms for over 220 industries. The estimates based on the (much smaller) GSOEP samples include separate constants for 35 industries.

CHAPTER 3

The Timing of Work

We have now examined the novel integration of time into days and daily hours of work in the United States and Germany, but we have not considered *when* work takes place. This chapter presents that analysis, paying most attention to studying work at the unusual times of evenings or nights, though with some additional information for the United States on the distribution of work over the entire day. This analysis of *instantaneous* time use should provide a novel view of the labor market, one that is not obtainable by looking at various integrations of time use, including the days-hours integration of the previous chapter.

A number of issues can only be studied using information on instantaneous time use. For example, what is the nature of spouses' joint demand for leisure at different times of the day? This issue is especially important for analyzing the demand for child care and the role of child-care subsidies. A huge literature has examined child care using integral time use data (e.g., Gustafsson and Stafford 1992). Surely, however, much of the difficulty in obtaining child care and using it to ease market activities arises because it is unavailable or expensive at times when the consumer/worker's own value of time in the market is highest. The effect of child care on the timing of work can only be understood properly with instantaneous data. Family decision making about work and leisure necessarily deals with questions about *when*, e.g., about who will work after 5PM, who will wake up to feed the baby at 3AM, etc. The general decision about how much to work may be integrative, but decisions about the specific issue of who will do what and when help to determine family well- being and are part of the bargaining that takes place within a marriage.

Popular demands for restructuring work clearly depend on how workers' marginal satisfactions in various activities differ at different points in time; and time use at each time of day or week depends on how workers' productivity differs at different moments. These are questions about instantaneous time use. Similarly, issues of retail opening hours are instantaneous: It matters greatly to workers whether stores are open the 40 hours per week 9AM to 5PM Monday through Friday, or the 40 hours that include noon to 6PM Monday through Saturday and 1PM to 5PM Sunday.

Instantaneous time use presents a wide variety of research topics (that, as I show below, have barely been touched by labor economists and others).[1] In this chapter I deal only with the determinants of the timing of work of individuals in the two countries in 1991 (1990 in Germany) and the role of timing of work within a marriage. The first section discusses the very meager previous research in this area; it is followed by an outline of the information available on this issue in the CPS and the GSOEP. The chapter then discusses patterns of timing using the individual worker as the basis of study, and then does the same thing using married couples as the central focus.

What Do We Know About Instantaneous Time Use?

Several well-known issues in the analysis of labor markets might be viewed as related to studying instantaneous time use. Substantial information has been produced on labor force participation, the zero-one question of whether a person is working or looking for work during a particular time interval (usually a week). This view could also be applied to analyzing whether or not the person works during a particular year on which one focuses. That example, however, would not be in the spirit of an approach to examining instantaneous time use, as work time clearly can take values other than zero or one over a basic interval that long. Indeed, even the standard focus of participation defined as occurring during a week necessarily masks a mix of leisure and work. Except for these somewhat inappropriate aspects, however, little theoretical or empirical research has been done on issues of instantaneous time use.

While there have been discussions of when people engage in different activities (for example, Melbin 1987), only Winston (1982) presents a theoretical analysis of time use at a particular instant of time. He discusses this from a variety of viewpoints, including that of the price-taking worker-consumer. We can view the typical worker as maximizing the present value of a stream of utility:

$$(3.1) \qquad U = \sum_{t=0}^{\infty} U^t(C^t, L^t, w^t, I)[1 + r]^{-t},$$

where $L^t = 0$ if the person is working during the short interval indexed by t, and 1 if not. C is consumption during any interval, w is the price of the worker's time during interval t, r is the worker's rate of time preference and I is unearned income. The crucial novelty in (3.1) is that the intervals are defined to be short enough so that the only economic decision is whether to work or to enjoy leisure (and consume). Disaggregating activities within the intervals is assumed to be physically impossible. The utility-maximizing sequence of L^t is chosen based upon how w^t and the shape of U^t vary over time. Specifying decision making this way becomes interesting to the extent that we can identify factors that affect w^t and U^t, the price of time during each interval and the worker's preferences about time use in that interval, and use them to make predictions about interpersonal differences in the sequences L^t.

The approach implicit in (3.1) treats the sequence w^t as exogenous. No doubt the worker has little control over the wages he or she is offered; but in a market context the wage rate is jointly determined by workers' tastes and labor productivity during each basic time interval.[2] Barzel's (1973) profound analysis of the relationship between daily schedules and wages, which incorporated issues of fatigue and productivity, recognized this jointness. While I make some effort to account for the effects of employers' behavior and to draw inferences as if some of the results stem from workers' behavior only, the nature of the instantaneous use of time as the output of an implicit market provides a caution on the interpretation of empirical results. Anything we observe about patterns of instantaneous time surely results from behavior by *both* workers and employers. Without a careful model estimated on matched establishment-household data, any findings are not solely expressions of workers' tastes for work at different times.

The sparseness of the theoretical development is matched by the near absence of empirical work on instantaneous time use. Some effort has been devoted to looking at shift work, including patterns in it (Hedges and Sekscenski 1979, and Mellor 1986), spouses' joint scheduling of shifts (Presser 1987) and cyclical changes in employers' demand for shift work (Mayshar and Solon 1993; Bresnahan and Ramey 1994). While the analysis of shift work may be interesting, it has much less to do with the study of instantaneous time use than one might think, as the data in table 3.1U should make clear. These data are based on the May 1991 Current Population Survey. The final column shows the percentage of all workers who are on a particular shift, while the first (second) column shows for each shift the percentage of all workers who are at work evenings (nights).

Table 3.1U   Percent Distributions of Workers by Shift and Timing of Work, 1991 (N = 56,781)

	Percent of Total Workforce:		
	At work 7PM-10PM	At work 10PM-6AM	Total on shift
Shift:			
Regular day	5.5	4.0	78.7
Regular evening	5.4	3.6	5.9
Regular night	1.3	3.0	3.1
Rotating	1.3	1.1	3.2
Split	.5	.2	1.0
Irregular	1.9	1.0	5.3
Other	1.1	.5	2.8
TOTAL	17.0	13.4	100.0

NOTE: Includes all workers who report four or more days of work in the survey week.

Table 3.1U classifies workers by shift according to the criteria of the U.S. Bureau of Labor Statistics (used by Mellor 1986). The overwhelming majority of workers put in regular day shifts. While relatively few of these people work evenings or nights, they are so numerous that they represent the largest percentages of evening and night workers. Indeed, the 5.4 percent of workers on regular evening shifts who work between 7 and 10PM account for only one-third of those at work in the evening. Regular night-shift workers account for less than one-fourth of those at work between 10PM and 6AM. Shift work tells us relatively little about the timing of work.[3]

Other researchers, including Wilson (1988) and Kostiuk (1990), examine variations in w^t over the workday (actually, only comparing variations across starting times or shifts). The evidence for the United States shows clearly that the premium for evening or night work is not large. Multiple job-holding, which is partly an issue of instantaneous time use, has also been studied (most recently by Krishnan 1990); and there has been some interest in how productivity varies over the workday (Hamermesh 1990), an issue that goes back to the underpinnings of Taylorism (Florence 1924). Pashigian and Bowen (1994) analyze how the rise in female labor force participation will change shopping patterns, but they do not consider households' use of time.[4] Only Hill (1988) studies the timing of labor supply (in the context of asking how spouses' simultaneous consumption of leisure is related to their subsequent likelihood of divorcing). There has, however, been no empirical analysis of scheduling decisions based on standard models of utility maximization. Indeed, we do not even know anything about the demographic correlates of workers' schedules.

Measuring the Timing of Work

The 1990 wave of the GSOEP provides information on whether the person works "nights after 10PM" or "evenings between 7PM and 10PM" in the three categories: "regularly," "occasionally," or "never." I assume, though it is not explicit in the questionnaire, that responses about evening or night work refer to what the worker does on most of the days when market work takes place.[5] The survey also asks if the individual had any Saturday (or Sunday) with employed work: every week; every 2 weeks; every 3-4 weeks; seldom; or never. The responses are elicited from the same set of questions that provided the information on days and daily hours of work that underlay the analysis in chapter 2. The questions seem to refer to work on the main job, so that I assume here that information refers to the work schedule on that job.[6]

The May 1991 Current Population Survey provides information on whether the individual was working on the main job on each particular day of the week (and offers similar information for any second job) and also asks for the starting and ending times on the main job (and on any second job). The CPS codes these starting and ending times as integral hours.[7] I thus construct for each respondent an index of whether he or she is at work at a particular hour in the day. Ideally we would like to have data on workers' schedules for each day in the workweek. Unfortunately, the questionnaire only asks for one day's schedule and does not make clear about which workday the respondent should be thinking when giving starting and ending times. Presumably people respond with their most frequent daily schedule. It would be very interesting to construct a profile of who is at work during each hour of the week; but because of the way this question is asked in the CPS Supplement, a respondent's schedule of daily work times cannot be linked to the days he or she is at work.

In some of the descriptive work in this chapter I present substantial temporal detail on instantaneous labor supply from the CPS. In order to maintain even limited comparability with the German data, however, I restrict most of the analysis of the CPS data to whether people are working at some point in the evening (7PM to 10PM) or at night (10PM to 6AM). Even with this restriction the obvious differences between the questions in the GSOEP and CPS mean that the results in this chapter are less comparable internationally than were the results on differences in patterns of days and daily hours of work in chapter 2. Because the distinction between main and all jobs is not so explicit in the GSOEP as it might be, many of the comparisons are made both to American data describing the main job, and the main job plus long (presumably at least several days per week) second jobs. As the evidence in table 2.1 made clear, this distinction is unlikely to be important.

The analysis in the following section is carried out on files of data describing time use by individual civilians in the sample. To analyze the timing of work by couples, I combine data for spouses from the May 1991 CPS to form a file that contains each spouse's and the household's demographic characteristics as well as the pattern of time use over the day and week by each spouse. From the GSOEP, I combine records for partners (married and unmarried) to create a similar file. These combinations generated the files of 30,936 married American couples and 2,651 opposite-sex German couples that form the basis for the analysis in the section on unusual work times.[8]

Before turning to the comparative analyses, we can use the data that I have constructed to allow an hour-by-hour profile of labor force activity in the United States. Given the framing of questions in the GSOEP on the timing of work, no analogous data for Germany can be constructed. Figure 3.1U presents this information for men and women separately based on time at work on the main job or on a second job (of at least 20 hours per week, so that it probably describes behavior on at least two workdays per week). (The relatively few people who work on long second jobs means that the same figure for time at work on the main job looks only slightly different.) It is the first available figure that presents this kind of information (though Hedges and Sekscenski 1979 did present distributions of starting and ending times separately).

Figure 3.1U   Work Time by Time of Day

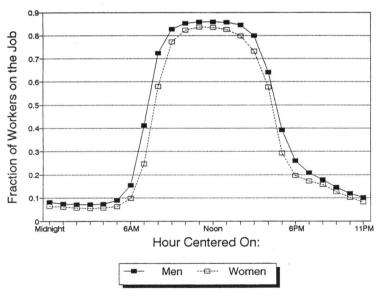

Most of the patterns are what we would expect. Most workers are on the job from 9AM through 4PM (at least 80 percent of male workers);

and at every single hour a greater fraction of male than of female workers are on the job, reflecting men's longer average daily hours. There is, however, no single hour when more than 87 percent of workers are at work. Obversely, even at the slackest time (3AM) at least 5 percent of male and female workers are engaged in market activity. In what follows I refer to work in the middle of the night as nonstandard or unusual, but it is not all that uncommon.

Patterns of Individuals' Work Time

This section examines work on weekends, and in the evening or at night, by individuals in the two countries. The purposes are to establish how important work at these unusual times is and to examine its correlates. As noted in the previous section, the differences between the nature of the information from Germany and the United States make international comparisons of the results somewhat difficult. Nonetheless, I do note the similarities and differences where they are interesting, especially where they serve to underscore the common determinants of labor market behavior.

Tables 3.2 give an overview of the extent of effort at these times in the two countries.[9] The upper half of each table presents information by gender for employees, and for the self-employed, on work on the weekend. The data are not completely comparable across countries, since the CPS asks about usual work patterns, while the GSOEP gives information on the frequency of work at nonstandard times. In what follows, I base the comparisons of the American data to weekend work in Germany performed each week or every other week, and to evening or night work in Germany performed regularly.

A surprisingly large fraction of employees works on Saturdays or Sundays in both countries. Nearly 20 percent of male American employees work on Saturdays, roughly equal to the percentage of Germans who work Saturdays at least every other week. Over 8 percent of male employees work on Sundays at least every other week in each country. While the patterns among male employees are very similar across countries, American women employees are much less likely to

Table 3.2U Percent Distributions of Workers by Timing of Work, 1991

	Employees		Self-employed
	Males	**Females**	
Saturday:			
Main job	19.9	13.9	42.9
Main job or second job	20.9	14.3	43.0
Sunday:			
Main job	8.2	6.5	17.5
Main job or second job	9.0	6.8	17.6
No weekend work:			
Main job	78.0	84.5	56.1
Main job or long second job	77.1	84.1	55.9
Regularly work:			
Some work 7-10PM:			
Main job	19.0	16.6	24.4
Main job or long second job	22.0	19.2	25.5
Some work 10PM-6AM:			
Main job	16.4	12.2	9.9
Main job or long second job	17.5	13.0	10.7
10PM-Midnight:			
Main job	12.9	10.6	6.9
Main job or long second job	13.9	11.4	7.5
Midnight-3AM:			
Main job	8.4	6.3	4.2
Main job or long second job	8.9	6.6	4.4
3-6AM:			
Main job	9.3	6.5	6.5
Main job or long second job	9.7	6.7	6.8
Only between 6AM and 7PM:			
Main job	75.8	80.4	73.6
Main job or long second job	72.7	77.8	72.3
N =	28,951	26,614	5,099

NOTE: Long second job at least 20 hours per week.

Table 3.2G   Percent Distributions of Workers by Timing of Work, 1990

| | Employees | | | | Self-employed | |
| | Males | | Females | | | |
Work on:	Sat.	Sun.	Sat.	Sun.	Sat.	Sun.
Each week	10.3	3.1	13.1	2.4	62.7	32.8
Every other week	12.6	5.6	11.8	6.7	10.5	4.2
Every 3-4 weeks	9.9	4.6	4.6	2.6	5.2	7.0
Seldom	11.0	6.2	4.4	2.6	4.9	11.5
Never	56.3	80.6	66.2	85.7	16.7	44.6
Infrequent or no weekend work	76.5		74.8		25.8	
N =	2903		1931		287	

Work:	7-10PM	After 10PM	7-10PM	After 10PM	7-10PM	After 10PM
Regularly	20.5	14.3	12.8	4.7	30.6	14.8
Occasionally	25.3	17.6	16.2	6.9	43.7	34.2
Never	54.2	68.1	70.9	88.5	25.7	51.1
No regular work between 6AM and 7PM	78.5		87.1		68.5	
N =	2879	2875	1917	1906	284	278

NOTE: May not add to 100 exactly due to rounding.

be working on Saturday than their German counterparts. Similarly, 9 percent of German women workers often work on Sundays, but fewer than 7 percent of American women do so.

Night work is also quite common in both countries, with one-fifth of male German employees regularly at work between 7PM and 10PM, and one-seventh regularly working between 10PM and 6AM. As with work on weekends, these figures are also remarkably close to those describing the incidence of evening and night work among American men. Among women the patterns do differ internationally, but in the opposite way from weekend work: German women are much less likely to work evenings or nights than their American counterparts. The difference in evening and night work may reflect the lesser participation rate and shorter hours of German female workers, as well as the formal opposition of German trade unions to women working at night. The more common weekend work by German women may result from married women's need to stay home during the week to care for children who are in school only half a day, a problem that does not exist on the weekend when in most German couples the husband is likely to be at home.

Self-employed workers, who presumably have greater freedom to choose the timing of their work, have strikingly different patterns of unusual work times from employees. The incidence of weekend work is greater in both countries than among employees, with self-employed workers being two to five times as likely to be working on Saturdays or Sundays. Among self-employed workers Germans are substantially more likely to work on weekends than their American counterparts, despite the legal limits imposed on self-employed owners of small retail shops. This difference reflects the longer workhours of a population of self-employed workers in Germany that, as noted in chapter 1, is about the same relative size as in the United States.

Since we saw in chapter 2 that the self-employed work more days, this table makes it clear that the margin of adjustment for those extra days is both Saturdays and Sundays. Tables 2.3 also showed that the self-employed work longer daily hours than employees. Tables 3.2 demonstrate that some of these extra hours are worked between 7PM and 10PM: the incidence of work is higher in both countries among the self-employed during this time period than among employees.

The evidence in tables 3.2 also makes it clear that, at least in the United States, the self-employed do not put in their extra hours worked at night: In each time interval between 10PM and 6AM the incidence of work is the same or lower among the self-employed than among employees. On the other hand, despite laws governing work by self-employed shopkeepers, the average German self-employed worker is more likely than his or her American counterpart to work occasionally after 10PM, and slightly more likely to work nights regularly. The American data show that night work is not so likely to be chosen by workers who are less constrained in timing their work. This result suggests that (American) workers use part of their ability to obtain additional earnings to "purchase" more attractive work times, and thus that labor force participants view working at night as, in economists' terms, "inferior."

The determinants of nonstandard work times are examined in the regressions reported in tables 3.3. In each pair the first table is for male workers and the second for females. In all four tables I present estimates with and without separate constants for the industry in which the respondent works. As in some of the regressions in chapter 2, for the United States this means that over 220 dummy variables, one for each three-digit Census industry, are included in the regressions reported. The German data provide enough information to allow the inclusion of separate constant terms for each of 35 industries.

The results for the United States are least-squares regressions on the zero-one variable, work in the evening (night) conditional on working at all.[10] To make the estimates for Germany comparable to those for the United States I define the zero-one variable, work regularly in the evening (night), in the German data and estimate least-squares regressions on this variable also. Since roughly the same percentage of Germans work regularly at these times as do Americans, this approach seemed to be the most useful way of combining the three responses in the GSOEP and making the results most comparable to those for the United States.

The construction of most of the other variables included in the regressions was discussed in chapter 2. Because the CPS contains substantial detail about the worker's place of residence, I also include in the equations a vector of variables indicating the size of the metropolitan statistical area (MSA) where the worker lives along with a vector of variables for region of residence. Data on location are not available in the public-use sample of the GSOEP, so that a comparison of these effects is not possible. The GSOEP does, however, contain information on the size of the firm where the worker is employed, and this is included in these equations.

We can view the results in the second and fourth columns of tables 3.3 as abstracting in part from interindustry differences in technology. These differences are important, as the substantial increases in the fractions of variance accounted for by these variables indicate. Also, accounting for industry effects allows us to interpret the estimates in columns (2) and (4) as reflecting supply behavior more than the estimates in columns (1) and (3). Holding constant the measures of firm size in the German results strengthens the interpretation of the effects of the other variables on the timing of work as resulting from workers' choices. Nonetheless, both sets of estimates should be viewed as being at least partly contaminated by the determinants of employers' behavior in the matching process of workers' preferences and employers' offers of schedules and associated wage rates.

More educated workers in the United States, and more educated men in Germany, are significantly less likely to be working evenings or at night. Better-educated German women, however, are more likely to work at these unusual times, though the effects are significant only for work at night. Except for this group, these results underscore a general finding throughout this and the next Section: Work at night is done disproportionately by workers with relatively little human capital. In the United States the government provides no special incentives that might lead employers to use low-skilled workers disproportionately on jobs that must be performed at night. In Germany this is less true, since wage premiums for night work escape the very high payroll tax rates on employers, and the total earnings taxed have a monthly ceiling.[11] Taken together, these results and considerations suggest that, especially in the United States, we may be fairly sure that the lower incidence of evening and night work among more educated workers reflects people's general desires not to work at such times and educated workers' use of their earning power to "purchase" work schedules at more desirable times. This is additional, strong evidence that people view work at night as inferior.

Table 3.3U1   OLS Estimates of Coefficients in the Determinants of the Probability of Working at Nonstandard Times, Main Job, 1991, Men, N=32,375

	7PM-10PM		10PM-6AM	
Probability:	.198		.158	
Years of schooling	-.0043	-.0018	-.0120	-.0095
	(.0008)	(.0009)	(.0007)	(.0008)
Age	-.0107	-.0037	.0031	.0032
	(.0010)	(.0010)	(.0009)	(.0009)
$Age^2/100$	.0103	.0023	-.0054	-.0051
	(.0011)	(.0011)	(.0011)	(.0011)
Age youngest child:				
0-5	.0224	.0188	-.0013	.0027
	(.0068)	(.0066)	(.0063)	(.0060)
>5	.0265	.0174	-.0177	-.0203
	(.0058)	(.0056)	(.0053)	(.0051)
Married	-.0483	-.0252	-.0089	-.0033
	(.0060)	(.0058)	(.0055)	(.0053)
Black	.0335	.0213	.0564	.0297
	(.0091)	(.0088)	(.0083)	(.0081)
Hispanic	-.0073	-.0249	-.0035	-.0085
	(.0094)	(.0091)	(.0086)	(.0083)
Area unemployment rate	-.0026	-.0022	.0048	.0024
	(.0014)	(.0014)	(.0013)	(.0012)
MSA > 2.5 million	-.0276	-.0124	-.0243	-.0215
	(.0061)	(.0061)	(.0055)	(.0056)
MSA .5-2.5 million	-.0178	-.0059	.0021	-.0014
	(.0060)	(.0060)	(.0055)	(.0055)
MSA < .5 million	-.0118	.0001	.0095	.0077
	(.0070)	(.0068)	(.0064)	(.0062)
Industry effects	No	Yes	No	Yes
$\bar{R}^2$	.020	.101	.016	.102

NOTE: Also included are dummy variables for major region, and for Asian or other racial group.

Table 3.3U2   OLS Estimates of Coefficients in the Determinants of the Probability of Working at Nonstandard Times, Main Job, 1991, Women, N=28,289

	7PM-10PM		10PM-6AM	
Probability:	.168		.120	
Years of schooling	-.0087	-.0016	-.0063	-.0019
	(.0009)	(.0010)	(.0008)	(.0009)
Age	-.0150	-.0096	.0027	.0026
	(.0010)	(.0010)	(.0009)	(.0009)
$Age^2/100$	.0147	.0092	-.0040	-.0034
	(.0012)	(.0012)	(.0011)	(.0011)
Age youngest child:				
0-5	.0293	.0184	.0183	.0075
	(.0068)	(.0065)	(.0060)	(.0058)
>5	.0040	-.0018	-.0129	-.0135
	(.0054)	(.0053)	(.0048)	(.0047)
Married	-.0601	-.0460	-.0339	-.0214
	(.0050)	(.0049)	(.0044)	(.0043)
Black	.0040	.0051	.0410	.0245
	(.0078)	(.0077)	(.0069)	(.0068)
Hispanic	-.0287	-.0228	-.0018	-.0001
	(.0098)	(.0095)	(.0086)	(.0084)
Area unemployment rate	.0008	.0001	.0015	.0007
	(.0014)	(.0014)	(.0012)	(.0012)
MSA > 2.5 million	-.0284	-.0137	-.0356	-.0235
	(.0061)	(.0060)	(.0054)	(.0053)
MSA .5-2.5 million	-.0107	-.0043	-.0189	-.0127
	(.0060)	(.0059)	(.0053)	(.0052)
MSA < .5 million	-.0118	-.0043	-.0134	-.0091
	(.0069)	(.0067)	(.0061)	(.0059)
Industry effects	No	Yes	No	Yes
$\overline{R}^2$	.035	.110	.009	.080

NOTE: Also included are dummy variables for major region, and for Asian or other racial group.

Table 3.3G1   OLS Estimates of Coefficients in the Determinants
of the Probability of Working Regularly
at Nonstandard Times, 1990, Men

	7PM-10PM		10PM-6AM	
Probability:	.215		.145	
Education	-.000015	-.000017	-.000015	-.000017
	(.000008)	(.000008)	(.000007)	(.000007)
Age	.0133	.0128	.0057	.0062
	(.0046)	(.0045)	(.0039)	(.0038)
Age^2/100	-.0180	-.0171	-.0082	-.0088
	(.0057)	(.0055)	(.0048)	(.0047)
Age youngest child:				
0-5	.0375	.0410	.0162	.0177
	(.0206)	(.0194)	(.0171)	(.0166)
>5	.0301	.0070	.0310	.0096
	(.0219)	(.0211)	(.0187)	(.0181)
Married	.0139	.0122	.0220	.0219
	(.0203)	(.0197)	(.0173)	(.0168)
Foreign-born	.0628	.0495	.0818	.0737
	(.0311)	(.0300)	(.0267)	(.0257)
Firm size:				
>2000 Employees	.1080	.1273	.1134	.1210
	(.0199)	(.0232)	(.0170)	(.0199)
200-1999 Employees	.0719	.0836	.0551	.0658
	(.0209)	(.0229)	(.0179)	(.0197)
20-199 Employees	-.0234	-.0020	-.0206	-.0062
	(.0209)	(.0219)	(.0179)	(.0187)
Industry effects	No	Yes	No	Yes
$\overline{R}^2$	.026	.107	.030	.112
N =	3187		3180	

Table 3.3G2   OLS Estimates of Coefficients in the Determinants of the Probability of Working Regularly at Nonstandard Times, 1990, Women

	7PM-10PM		10PM-6AM	
Probability:	.135		.053	
Education	.000009	.000006	.000013	.000012
	(.000007)	(.000007)	(.000005)	(.000005)
Age	.0051	.0044	.0061	0056
	(.0048)	(.0046)	(.0031)	(.0031)
Age^2/100	-.0070	-.0065	-.0078	-.0074
	(.0060)	(.0059)	(.0040)	(.0039)
Age youngest child:				
0-5	.0362	.0345	.0113	.0086
	(.0220)	(.0214)	(.0144)	(.0142)
>5	-.0029	-.0195	.0125	.0019
	(.0210)	(.0203)	(.0139)	(.0136)
Married	-.0148	-.0185	-.0046	-.0053
	(.0180)	(.0173)	(.0118)	(.0115)
Foreign-born	.0076	-.0013	.0082	.0054
	(.0312)	(.0301)	(.0206)	(.0200)
Firm size:				
>2000 Employees	.0286	.0880	.0281	.0459
	(.0214)	(.0239)	(.0141)	(.0159)
200-1999 Employees	.0673	.0987	.0113	.0265
	(.0200)	(.0216)	(.0132)	(.0144)
20-199 Employees	.0022	.0277	-.0211	-.0100
	(.0192)	(.0201)	(.0126)	(.0134)
Industry effects	No	Yes	No	Yes
$\overline{R}^2$	.005	.093	.007	.075
N =	2155		2140	

The interesting international distinctions arise in the relation between age and the probability of working evenings or at night. The probability of evening work falls for American men and women until roughly age fifty and rises thereafter. This is consistent with the effect of education on working at night, as workers whose investments in themselves are greater "buy" a more desirable work schedule. The probability of night work shows the opposite pattern, rising for both genders in the United States, though only until workers reach their early thirties, and then falling. In Germany the patterns of both evening and night work are the same: the probability initially rises with age, reaches peaks in workers' mid-thirties, then begins to drop. The results are roughly the same whether or not we hold constant for the worker's industry.[12]

The relationship of age to night work in the United States and to evening and night work in Germany is inconsistent with simple human-capital theory. These apparently contradictory results could arise if the pay premium for night work in the United States (for both evening and night work in Germany) were sufficiently high to offset people's unwillingness to be at work at the unusual times. Given the somewhat relevant evidence that shift differentials are relatively small in the United States, probably 10 percent on average, and not more than 20 percent at the margin (Kostiuk 1990; Shapiro 1995), this explanation is not very satisfactory for the United States. While no econometric studies have examined this issue for Germany, typical union contracts (which cover the much larger unionized sector in Germany and whose provisions are often extended to nonunion workers) suggest roughly similar premia.[13] Insofar as the probability even of night work is lower at age 50 in these groups than at age 25, however, the results can still be viewed as being consistent with life-cycle behavior, though not with the predicted U-shaped relationship to age.

The GSOEP allows us to explore an additional facet of the allocation of evening and night work, as it provides information on workers' tenure with their employer. A vector of variables indicating tenure was added to the equations, but none of the estimated coefficients in any of the four equations was significantly different from zero. Moreover, the inclusion of these vectors did not alter the pattern of coefficients on the age variables. This suggests that it is the life-cycle effects of preferences, not the interaction of seniority and the concomitant firm-specific investment with those preferences, that determines who works at these times.

Hispanic workers do not differ greatly from non-Hispanic whites in their propensity to work at unusual times; but black workers of both genders are significantly more likely than non-Hispanic whites to be at work evenings or nights. Part of this difference disappears when the worker's detailed industry is held constant. Even accounting for this level of detail on industry, however, racial differences remain significant and fairly substantial. For example, among black women the probability of night work is 25 percent higher than among non-Hispanic whites within the same narrowly defined industry. One might argue that this racial differential reflects lower-quality schooling (for a given number of years of education attained); but the relatively small impact of low schooling on the probability of evening and night work invalidates that argument. The race differential in evening and night work seems either to reflect a difference in tastes, which is hard to believe, or to be the outcome of labor market discrimination.

The outcomes for foreign-born workers in Germany parallel the results for blacks in the United States. Foreign-born German men are significantly more likely to be working evenings or nights than are native German workers, while for women the effects are generally positive but never significant. In both countries the burden of working at nonstandard times is greater on minorities.

Interarea differences in unemployment are not strongly associated with differences in the probability of working evenings or nights. That is not true, however, for the vector of variables in table 3.3U indicating the size of the metropolitan area where the worker resides. In the equations that contain detailed industry effects this vector should be interpreted as reflecting the marginal impact of workers' disutility associated with being outside the house in areas of different size. The parameters on the variables for medium and smaller MSAs are generally negative, though not significantly so in the equations describing the probability of working evenings. In the equations for the probability of night work they are significantly negative for women.

The most interesting result is that residence in the largest MSAs significantly reduces the probability of evening work among both women and men; and for both genders the probability of night work is significantly lower there, with a slightly bigger effect among women. These differences exist even within detailed industries.[14] Thus unless *intra*industry differences in the relative difficulty of producing in the evening or at night are associated with location, this pattern of results is consistent with workers' greater unwillingness to venture out to work in the dark where the perceived danger of being away from home is greater, with women apparently slightly more concerned about these dangers.

The data do not permit replication of this result for Germany. Tables 3.3G do, however, allow us to infer that evening and night work are more prevalent in larger firms, especially for men. This is not just the result of differences in technology across industries: The effects are actually a bit larger when we hold constant for two-digit industry (in columns (2) and (4)). One might argue that larger firms are more capital-intensive and that workers must labor in the evening and at night to keep the valuable equipment occupied. If that were true, however, we would find that the coefficients on firm size, particularly for very large firms, decline once the dummy variables for industry are added to the equations. That the coefficients remain essentially unchanged or even rise suggests that this effect is generated by workers' supply behavior. In a spirit similar to the explanation for the results on city size in the United States, the positive correlation of firm size and evening and night work in Germany may reflect people's greater willingness to work where there is a greater likelihood that more co-workers will be present.

Married American men are significantly less likely to be working evenings than are single men, though only slightly and insignificantly less likely to be working nights. Among German men marital status is positively, though not significantly, related to the probability of work at nonstandard times. In both Germany and the United States married women are less likely to be working evenings and nights, though only for American women are the effects significant (and both absolutely and proportionally larger than for American men). This might, of course, merely reflect married women's generally lower supply of hours in both countries.

What is surprising is that women with small children are more likely than those with no children to work evenings and nights, with the effects being significant in the United States. This is not the result of differences in behavior between single and married mothers, since including interactions between marital status and children did not alter this inference.

Since the best-documented fact about female labor supply is that the presence of small children reduces total hours of work, this finding implies that mothers of young children concentrate a disproportionate part of their market work outside what are considered standard working hours.[15] Moreover, this concentration is independent of any differences in child-care arrangements between the two countries.

Unusual Work Times in a Family Context

While the above results for young mothers are intriguing, they are basically not satisfying. Without analyzing how couples use time *jointly,* we cannot infer how alternative family situations affect the instantaneous probabilities of alternative uses of time. There is evidence that older couples treat aggregations of leisure time as complements (Hamermesh 1980, chapter 4); but the more general labor supply literature has difficulty finding effects in formal models of spouses' labor supply based on data on integral time use (Killingsworth and Heckman 1986). By negative example these findings illustrate the importance of considering instantaneous time use: given the relatively small fractions of the week that people typically work, we could very easily find that husbands' longer weekly hours are associated with wives' longer weekly hours, holding their wage rates constant, even though each one is at home while the other works. The issue is not whether total work times of husband and wife are correlated when we integrate over a day, a week, or a year. It is whether at each instant the probabilities that husband and wife are at work are independent.

Some inkling into the jointness of a couple's use of time *at a point in time* is obtained from simple contingency tables. Tables 3.4 include all married couples regardless of whether both spouses work or only one does. Each shows the percentage of couples choosing each of the four possible outcomes for work at the nonstandard times (7PM-10PM and 10PM-6AM), along with the probability of observing this pattern of outcomes (based on the appropriate χ^2 test). For both countries the first tableau in each table makes it clear that among couples without children the instantaneous time use of husbands and wives is complementary: if one partner is working at a nonstandard time, the other is more likely to be at work.

Table 3.4U **Contingency Tables on Spouses' Work Time by Age**
of Youngest Child, 1991, Percent Distributions,
All Married Couples

		7PM-10PM		10PM-6AM	
		Woman works:		Woman works:	
No kids		N	Y	N	Y
	N	85.94	4.18	89.36	3.08
Man works:					
	Y	7.92	1.96	6.27	1.29
N = 16,659		p = .000		p = .000	
		Woman works:		Woman works:	
Youngest 6-17		N	Y	N	Y
	N	77.92	6.07	81.91	5.44
Man works:					
	Y	13.70	2.30	11.08	1.58
N = 7,428		p = .000		p = .000	
		Woman works:		Woman works:	
Youngest 3-5		N	Y	N	Y
	N	73.32	7.50	78.95	6.00
Man works:					
	Y	16.29	2.89	13.58	1.46
N = 2,732		p = .000		p = .058	
		Woman works:		Woman works:	
Youngest 0-2		N	Y	N	Y
	N	72.21	7.48	78.46	5.66
Man works:					
	Y	17.56	2.74	14.28	1.60
N = 4,117		p = .000		p = .002	
		Woman works:		Woman works:	
Youngest 0-5		N	Y	N	Y
	N	72.65	7.49	78.65	5.80
Man works:					
	Y	17.05	2.80	14.00	1.55
N = 6,849		p = .000		p = .000	

Table 3.4G   Contingency Tables on Couples' Work Time by Age of Youngest Child, 1990, Percent Distributions, All Opposite-Sex Couples

		Married Couples			
		7PM-10PM		**After 10PM**	
		Woman works:		Woman works:	
No kids		N	Y	N	Y
Man works:	N	80.07	3.53	88.04	1.00
	Y	13.77	2.63	9.33	1.63
N = 1104		p = .000		p = .000	
		Woman works:		Woman works:	
Youngest 6-16		N	Y	N	Y
Man works:	N	72.14	5.98	81.71	2.39
	Y	5.98	2.56	14.70	1.20
N = 585		p = .146		p = .026	
		Woman works:		Woman works:	
Youngest 0-5		N	Y	N	Y
Man works:	N	72.05	3.84	83.29	1.78
	Y	22.33	1.78	14.52	.41
N = 730		p = .242		p = .665	
		Unmarried couples			
		Woman works:		Woman works:	
		N	Y	N	Y
Man works:	N	76.72	9.91	82.76	8.62
	Y	9.91	3.45	8.62	0
N = 232		p = .029		p = .151	

NOTE: Regular work during these times.

As the second tableau for the United States shows, and as is true for night work in Germany, couples consume leisure jointly (work at the same time) when the youngest child in the house is of school age. When the youngest German child is a preschooler, however, husbands' and wives' leisure choices in the evening and at night are independent. With the much larger samples in the United States we still find some jointness in the consumption of leisure at night (when the young child is likely to be asleep); but for couples with young children the outcomes of choices about work and leisure in the (weekday) evening are somewhat less closely related. Together the evidence shows that the presence of young children loosens the nexus between the husband's and wife's joint consumption of leisure.[16]

The final tableau in table 3.4G shows that unmarried opposite-sex German couples behave differently from married ones without children: patterns of leisure are less mutually dependent among unmarried couples. This suggests that, as we would expect, each unmarried partner's choices are less based in maximizing utility jointly with the other partner than are the choices of spouses.

These tables suggest that partners wish to consume leisure jointly and that young children reduce this jointness; but to analyze the issue we need to abstract from factors that might affect the spouses' total demands for leisure and consumption over some integral of time. I thus hold constant each spouse's total work time and the couple's total consumption (actually, income), all of which are determined simultaneously by the interaction of the partners' wage rates and unearned income with the family utility function. This allows the analysis to focus on those factors that affect patterns of instantaneous work or leisure activity of the husband and wife after accounting for decisions about total work effort. As long as the premiums for work at different times of the day are the same for all labor force participants, any nonrandom patterns must result from the couple's preferences or from differences in the value of each spouse's nonmarket time at different times of the day. This approach thus allows us to concentrate on the single issue of joint instantaneous time use and to avoid the usual (and increasing) econometric complexities involved in analyzing temporal aggregates of labor supply. This is possible if we restrict the analysis to couples with both partners working. Including a spouse whose labor supply is zero means we could not infer whether the spouses view their leisure as joint substitutes at a point in time, or merely whether there is some unobserved heterogeneity that generates a greater probability of one spouse working at a particular time that is related to the couple's choice that the other spouse not work at all.

Only married couples with both spouses reporting positive days and hours of work are therefore included in the analysis of the joint consumption of leisure. I divide the couples into the four categories implicit in the contingency tables in tables 3.4 and estimate the effects of family structure using a multinomial logit procedure in which the excluded category is that neither spouse is at work during the particular time interval under study. The parameter estimates thus show the impact of a one-unit increase in the independent variable on the log odds of choosing a particular category (e.g., wife works, husband does not) relative to the probability that neither spouse works at that time. Each spouse's days and hours per day of work are included in the logits, so that I am inquiring into how people shift the timing of their leisure within a fixed total amount of leisure consumed. Also included in the equations for the United States, but not presented in table 3.5U, are the vector of variables denoting the size of the worker's metropolitan area (as included in table 3.3U) and indicators of the household head's race and ethnicity. In the estimates for Germany, I include an indicator of whether the household head is foreign-born.

The purpose of this careful set of controls is to analyze how the four possible choices are affected by the presence of children and by a family's full income. The former are represented by variables measuring the age of the youngest child (less than 6 years, 6-17 (16 in Germany), or no child under 18 (17 in Germany) at home, the excluded category). The couple's family income is reported in the GSOEP as monthly income and in the CPS as annual income.[17] Including income in the logits is a pure test of income effects on couples' relative demand for jointly consuming leisure at various times of the day, since their days and hours of work are held constant. The sample is quite large for the United States (N = 13,266), but fairly small for Germany (N = 1050), which means that the number of German couples in some of the categories (e.g., children under 6 and only the wife working at night) is unfortunately very small.

Table 3.5G is based on time at work, possibly work on any job. To ensure that we have one set of outcomes that reflects all labor at these

Table 3.5U Determinants of the Timing of Joint Labor Supply, Married Couples with Both Spouses Working, 1991, All Jobs (Multinomial Logit Estimates)

	Time at Work:					
	7PM-10PM			10PM-6AM		
	(2)	(3)	(4)	(6)	(7)	(8)
	Wife only	Husband only	Both	Wife only	Husband only	Both
Probability:	.097	.156	.049	.077	.125	.031
Youngest child:						
0-5	.550	.253	.052	.621	.259	-.129
	(.074)	(.063)	(.101)	(.084)	(.067)	(.127)
>5	.144	.006	-.433	.408	.065	-.317
	(.074)	(.060)	(.102)	(.082)	(.065)	(.122)
Annual income (000)	-.0076	-.0053	-.0104	-.0089	-.0093	-.0086
	(.0012)	(.0009)	(.0016)	(.0013)	(.0010)	(.0020)
Pseudo-R^2		.047			.037	
N =		13,266			13,266	
Tests of constraints: (p-values on χ^2-statistics)						
Kids matter:		.0000			.0000	
Kids (2) (or (6)) = Kids (3) (or (7)):		.0041			.0003	

NOTE: Neither spouse working at this time is the excluded category. Each spouse's hours and days worked are also included in the estimation. The household head's race and ethnicity (Hispanic or not) and the size of the metropolitan area where the couple resides are also held constant in both multinomial logits.

Table 3.5G Determinants of the Timing of Joint Labor Supply, Married Couples with Both Spouses Working, 1990 (Multinomial Logit Estimates)

	Time at Work:					
	7PM-10PM			10PM-6AM		
	(2)	(3)	(4)	(6)	(7)	(8)
	Wife only	Husband only	Both	Wife only	Husband only	Both
Probability:	.104	.151	.051	.028	.118	.025
Youngest child:						
0-5	.994	.371	.501	.810	.238	-.082
	(.269)	(.228)	(.362)	(.523)	(.252)	(.527)
>5	.752	.380	.305	.791	.416	.024
	(.271)	(.218)	(.370)	(.524)	(.237)	(.481)
Monthly income (000)	.076	-.019	-.049	.016	-.118	-.082
	(.035)	(.052)	(.095)	(.060)	(.069)	(.126)
Pseudo-R^2		.061			.102	
N =		1050			1050	
Tests of constraints: (p-values on χ^2-statistics)						
Kids matter:		.004			.426	
Kids (2) (or (6)) = Kids (3) (or (7)):		.162			.593	

NOTE: Neither spouse working at this time is the excluded category. Each spouse's hours and days worked are also included in the estimation. Foreign birth is held constant instead of race and ethnicity measures, and no measures of the size of the area are included.

unusual times and to make the results more comparable across countries, Table 3.5U includes all time worked on the main job or on a major second job between 7PM and 10PM or 10PM and 6AM. The results are affected only minutely if the sample underlying table 3.5U is restricted to work on the main job at unusual times.

As implied by the contingency tables in tables 3.4, having children at home significantly affects the pattern of spouses' consumption of leisure at these unusual work times in the United States and has similar effects, though ones that are insignificant for night work, in Germany. Relative to the probability that neither spouse works at an unusual time, children increase the likelihood that only one spouse will be at work at such times *conditional on the total days and hours supplied by each spouse.* In the United States, young children have insignificant effects on the relative probabilities that both spouses will be working in the evening or at night compared to the probability that neither works at this nonstandard time. Having older children at home, however, significantly reduces the chance that both partners will be at work evenings or nights. Whether this stems from a desire to consume leisure jointly with the older children or from concerns about what the children will do with their unsupervised leisure is unclear. In Germany having children at home does not significantly affect the relative probability that both partners work at night.

The data, especially the GSOEP, allow us to examine a number of interesting extensions of the basic model. One possibility is that the results are confounded by their ignoring the role that other household members might play in child care. Reestimating the multinomial logits for the United States with the inclusion of a variable indicating the presence of another adult in the household (present in 18 percent of the households underlying these estimates), we find no qualitative differences in the results shown in table 3.5U. Similarly, when the equations for Germany are reestimated to include an indicator of whether having an adult relative living with the couple affects the outcomes, none of the basic conclusions is changed.

Little more can be done on the American data; but the richer German data enable us to examine a number of other possibilities. One is to consider whether couples' beliefs about the role of the very stringent laws regulating retail hours in Germany are related to their choices of nonstandard work times. Despite the relatively short retail hours in Germany, couples responding in the questionnaire that lengthening retail hours would be important or very important do not exhibit significantly different patterns of nonstandard work times from other couples.

Among German couples using formal child-care arrangements, both spouses are slightly less likely to be working evenings or nights, with the only significant difference being that use of formal child care is less common if both spouses are working at night. Given the relative rarity of formal child-care opportunities in the former West Germany, it is not surprising that these effects are small.[18] People who indicate that they would like to obtain alternative child-care arrangements, however, do behave significantly differently from others. The husband is less likely to be working at night while his wife is at home; and both spouses are less likely to be working in the evening. An interpretation of this result (and the standard problem with such subjective responses) is that couples who view the issue as important are those who are least satisfied with the current arrangement, and in this case implicitly are those who cannot choose work times as freely as other couples with children.

An interesting question is whether the presence of young children, who we showed increase the probability that one partner works evenings or nights, is more likely to cause the husband or the wife to be working at these unusual times. The final p-values in the tables are based on tests of the hypothesis that the effects of children (under 6, or 6 and over) are symmetric on which spouse is at work at an unusual time while the other is at home. In the United States they are not: it is the wife who shifts her workhours toward these nonstandard times while the husband stays home with the (sleeping?) child. For Germany the test statistics are not significantly nonzero, but the differences in the relative effects are in the same directions as in the United States.[19]

One explanation for these results is that wives spend more time at home with the children during the day, so that their enjoyment from still more time with them is less than that of their husbands. Alternatively, though it seems farfetched, it is possible that the wage premium that wives receive for work at these unusual times compared to standard work times is greater than that of their husbands. In any case, it is clear that for workweeks of given lengths (same days and daily hours), the *timing* of mothers' work is more affected by the presence of children than is that of fathers.

In Germany higher income reduces the probability that both spouses or the husband alone work at nonstandard times, though none of the effects is significantly negative. In the United States there is, however, a significant negative income effect on all three alternatives to being at home together in the evening or at night. While the effects on the three combinations that involve evening work by one or both spouses are significantly different from each other in the United States (with the biggest negative effect on evening work by both spouses), higher income reduces night work in the United States by the same percentage for each category of outcome. The immense array of results from the labor supply literature has convinced us that the demand for leisure over an aggregate of time rises if people are given income independent of the amount they work. Taken together the results here demonstrate that a married couple's demand for jointly consuming leisure at a point in time is affected similarly.

Tables 3.5 do not list the impacts of additional workdays or daily hours of each spouse on their patterns of night and evening work; but in light of the findings in chapter 2 on the differences in the patterns and correlates of days and daily hours, it is interesting to inquire how these integral measures relate to couples' patterns of labor supply at nonstandard times. The evidence is very clear on this: (1) Working more days or more daily hours has only a weak relationship to working in the evening or at night among married labor force participants; and (2) Unsurprisingly, additional daily hours are more strongly positively related to work at nonstandard times than are additional days of work. Even here, however, the relationship is not very pronounced.

Conclusions and Implications

In this chapter I have introduced the empirical analysis of instantaneous time use—whether workers are in the labor market during particular narrow time intervals. This line of research should be distinguished from the analysis of integrative time use—hours, days, weeks, etc.—that is the focus of chapter 2, the first part of chapter 4, and chapter 5 of this monograph and of nearly all research on labor supply. The more important findings on instantaneous time use are:

> Work in the evening or at night is inferior. The self-employed, who presumably are more free to choose their own schedules, are less likely to be at work at night, even though their total weekly hours exceed those of employees. Among married couples with identical days and hours of work, those with higher incomes are less likely to be in the labor market at these times. Blacks in the United States and foreign-born workers in Germany are more likely than otherwise identical workers to be in the labor market at these nonstandard work times independent of the industry where they work.

> Husbands and wives without children at home are in or out of the labor market at the same times of the day. The jointness is less among couples with school-age children, and it nearly disappears when very young children are present.

> Even though women are much less likely than men to work nights and evenings, they bear a disproportionate share of the extra burden of such work when young children are present.

> Evening and night work are least prevalent in our largest cities, an effect that is slightly more pronounced among women workers.

Like the results in chapter 2 on the unusual temporal aggregates, these findings suggest the importance of child-care facilities in determining working time, especially that of women workers. That having young children leads mothers to alter their work schedules is not a problem; but it induces a shift toward those unusual work times that women generally do not like and that workers' behavior suggests are inferior. Either couples do not have access to sufficiently low-priced child-care facilities that would enable them to avoid these work times, or regardless of price women particularly wish to be with their young children during daytime and must work at night if they are to work at all.

If the German data provided more detail on timing rather than merely on evening and night work, it would have been possible to compare the timing of work in the two countries more broadly. Had the U.S. survey asked for each person's usual schedule on each day we could have derived a complete picture of who is at work when. Despite the drawbacks of the data, however, the analyses summarized here have generated new results about labor force behavior. This is not surprising, as it is easy to do so if new, albeit not totally satisfactory, snapshots are taken of working time.

NOTES

1. While there has been little analysis of these, Owen (1979) recognized their importance and discussed them at some length.

2. As Stafford (1980) points out, variations in labor productivity over the work schedule depend in part on the jointness of the schedules of capital and labor. This is especially important where the capital stock is lumpy and is specialized in a particular use.

3. While the table is restricted to those who work at least four days per week, the distributions look very similar if all workers are included.

4. Laband and Heinbuch (1987) discuss some of the issues involved in retail opening hours and how government regulations affect them.

5. I also assume, based on discussions with Professor Gert Wagner of the Deutsches Institut für Wirtschaftsforschung, who is responsible for the survey, that work at night after 10PM means work between 10PM and 6AM.

6. The instructions tell the respondent, "… beantworten Sie die folgenden Fragen bitte nur für Ihre derzeitige berufliche Haupttätigkeit." ("… please answer the following questions only for your current main paid activity.")

7. Clearly there is a problem in assigning starting and ending times to a particular single hour. In the CPS tapes the convention is to code any time between 30 minutes before the hour and 29 minutes after as being that hour only. Thus people who say their work starts at 7:45AM and ends at 6:23PM would be coded as starting at 8AM and finishing at 6PM.

8. In the CPS, I merged records from files of adult men and women who were listed as residing in a household in which both spouses were present. This resulted in successful matches of 97.3 percent of married men and 95.7 percent of married women. Combining individuals is especially easy in the GSOEP, as each individual record lists the partner's unique identification number, so that every person who listed a partner could be matched to that partner. The process of combining records in the GSOEP generated a small number of same-sex couples. Whether these really are homosexual couples or simply same-sex people domiciled together is unclear. Since in any case their behavior is likely to differ from that of the rest of the combined sample, I drop them from the analysis.

9. The numbers of observations for evening and night work differ slightly in the GSOEP because a few workers who responded to the question about Saturday work did not respond about their Sunday work, and vice-versa.

10. Clearly, probit analysis is the correct econometric procedure. A few were estimated, with coefficients that implied the same effects at the mean as the least-squares coefficients in tables 3.3 and with almost identical t-statistics.

11. Einkommensteuergesetz 1990, Gruppe 1.

12. Without data on the health status of each worker in these samples we cannot be sure that the tapering off of work at night after the late forties is not based on declining health. Many other studies suggest, however, that differences in health status by age are very minor at least until the late fifties, so that health problems do not seem to be a good explanation for patterns of nonstandard work by age.

13. For example, the contract covering the chemical industry beginning in June 1992 specified a premium of 15 percent for regular night work and 20 percent if the night work is performed on an irregular basis. (Manteltarifvertrag für die chemische Industrie vom 24. Juni 1992).

14. None of the effects discussed here changes if we restrict the samples by excluding those few workers who are enrolled in school.

15. This may also be the *only* commonly agreed upon fact generated by the immense econometric literature on female labor supply.

16. Excerpts from author's conversation with flight attendants on April 18, 1994, somewhere between Washington and Dallas:

Lisa: My husband has an 8 to 5 job. I bid weekday trips so we can be together. We don't have any kids yet.

Teri: I want to be with my babies, so I bid weekend trips.

17. The GSOEP gives monthly income in Deutschmarks, with a ceiling of 75,000DM per month (equivalent to an annual income of nearly $650,000 at the exchange rates of summer 1995). I multiplied 75,000DM by 1.5 and assigned that value to the one couple that listed the top code. In the CPS the responses on income are categorical and describe annual income. Midpoints of the categories were assigned; and for those at the topcoded amount of $75,000 I again multiplied by 1.5 and assigned that number to the respondents. Clearly, topcoding is not a problem in the German data. In the U.S. data, however, 13.6 percent of the married couples with both spouses working that are used in the analysis in table 3.5U were topcoded.

18. Only 3 percent of children below the age of 3 have access to such facilities. Of 3-5 year-olds 69 percent do, but only 5 percent of schoolchildren age 6-10 have the opportunity to obtain a place in a child-care facility (Schettkat and Fuchs 1994).

19. In the United States even the absolute effects are greater, while in Germany they are about the same. The conclusions are not changed if we restrict the samples only to those couples where at least one spouse is working in the evening (or at night). Even among such couples, in both countries that partner will disproportionately be the wife.

CHAPTER 4

How Work Schedules Change

Chapters 2 and 3 generated a novel set of results about the correlates of work schedules. We have learned much about how days and daily hours vary across the workforce in the two countries, and how patterns of evening and night work relate to demographic and economic characteristics. Those are, though, only correlates; and chapters 2 and 3 demonstrated these results only at a point in time. Days and daily hours, and work schedules generally, result from the interactions of workers' (varied) tastes with firms' (varied) technologies. In chapter 5 we make an effort to consider these outcomes from what one might view as the demand side of the labor market. First, however, we can use the same basic household data that underlay the empirical results in chapters 2 and 3 to attempt to distinguish the roles of workers' and employers' behavior in determining scheduling outcomes by considering how people's patterns of work time change over time.

The most important question to be answered here is the extent to which workers' desires for a change in schedules can be met by their current employers. When their situations change, is the workplace flexible enough to accommodate that change, or must the workers look elsewhere for a schedule that matches their altered tastes? More important, is it days or daily hours that workers find harder to vary within their current workplaces? Can the timing of work during the day be changed readily within the workplace, or are the same workers stuck working at undesirable times for many years in a row?

In many cases some demographic event—a marriage, a divorce, the birth of a child—leads workers and their families to recognize that a different schedule is now more desirable. How do these demographic changes alter the worker's schedule? Does this alteration occur in the context of the same job, or must the worker leave in order to find a job that meets the new desiderata?

Chapter 3 demonstrated that work in the evenings and at nights is "inferior" in the sense that it is not something chosen by people who can command greater earnings—the educated, majority workers, and others. Does this mean, however, that individual uneducated and minority workers are condemned to a (work) lifetime at nonstandard hours? To examine this we need to look at the degree to which individual workers flow in and out of different daily work schedules.

This chapter examines these questions using data from the GSOEP for 1990 and 1992, and from the Current Population Surveys of May 1977 and May 1978. The first section presents an outline of the theory of the determination of days and daily hours on a job and how they might be altered to match workers' changing circumstances, and it proposes some ways to measure the extent to which days and hours are fixed within a particular job. The next section describes the construction of the data sets that I use to examine how days, daily hours and the daily timing of work change when workers' circumstances change. The analysis of days and daily hours in these German and American data is then presented, followed by some estimates (for the United States only) of how the timing of workers' daily schedules changes from one year to the next.

Changes in Days and Hours Within and Across Jobs

Consider a schedule of days and daily hours offered on some job by a particular employer. We can denote that schedule by the pair (D^*, H^*), where the asterisk indicates that the quantity represents the firm's profit-maximizing values of days and hours, *given* how people's supply prices—their wage rates, W—change as D and H change. While these choices of workdays and daily hours maximize the firm's profits given wages, the firm may still be willing to employ a worker on a different schedule. If the firm alters a worker's schedule, the change in its profits depends on: (1) how steeply output falls off with departures from D^* and from H^*; and (2) how willing (and able) workers are to cut wages as days and hours depart from the previously optimally matched values, D^* and H^*.

Assume that something shocks the worker's preferences for work schedules, so that the pair (D^*, H^*) is no longer the most desired choice (given the wage rate associated with that combination). The response to this shock, in terms of any change in D and H, depends on how easily W can be altered compared to the work schedule. Assume that changing W is very difficult, perhaps because other workers object to one of their colleagues taking a wage cut to work a different schedule and respond by reducing their own effort. If the worker has no ties to the firm in the form of firm-specific human capital, the optimal solution for both parties is for the worker to separate (whether by layoff or quit is irrelevant) and find another job that can accommodate the changed preferences about work schedules. On the new job, at a firm whose profits reach a maximum at the worker's new desired combination of workdays and daily hours, the worker attains his or her desired work schedule at the highest wage rate available in the market. Given the shock to preferences that has occurred, this job change is optimal.

In reality workers have ties to their employers that provide the latter with some incentive to alter work schedules when the workers' circumstances change. The cost of this alteration depends on how sharply output decreases when days are altered from D^* and daily hours from H^*. For a given (unobservable) specific value of the worker-firm match, the firm is less likely to alter days as compared to hours the more costly (in terms of production) is the alteration. If changing workdays from D^* is very expensive at the margin relative to changing daily hours from H^*, we would observe that workers who separate (take new jobs) alter their days worked substantially compared to workers who stay with the employer. Changes in hours per day, on the other hand, would differ little between workers who remain with their employers and those who switch jobs, because they would be easy to alter on the current job. By comparing changes in days and daily hours between workers who leave their jobs and those who remain, we can obtain structural information on the ease with which firms can alter different aspects of their offered schedules (assuming, as seems reasonable, that a worker's willingness and ability to take a wage cut are the same in response to changing desires for days of work as they are to changing preferences for daily hours).

Reporting errors guarantee that workers will state that they have changed days or daily hours on a job even if the true work schedule has not changed. We cannot abstract from that in the subsequent analysis and must assume that this sort of "noise" pervades all the measures of changes. We can, however, calculate the difference between the variance of changes in scheduled days among workers who change jobs (N) and the same variance among workers who remain on their old jobs (O) as:

$$(4.1)\quad \Delta\sigma^2(\mathrm{d}\ln D) = \sigma^2_N(\mathrm{d}\ln D) - \sigma^2_O(\mathrm{d}\ln D),$$

where (dln) denotes the percentage change over some period of time. This difference can be compared to the analogous difference describing percentage changes in daily hours:

$$(4.2)\quad \Delta\sigma^2(\mathrm{d}\ln H) = \sigma^2_N(\mathrm{d}\ln H) - \sigma^2_O(\mathrm{d}\ln H).$$

Given the assumptions about the equal responsiveness of wages to changes in D and H, a larger positive difference in the differences in the schedules:

$$(4.3)\quad \Delta^2 S = \Delta\sigma^2(\mathrm{d}\ln D) - \Delta\sigma^2(\mathrm{d}\ln H),$$

would show that scheduled days are relatively more difficult to change within jobs than are scheduled daily hours.[1]

The discussion suggested that the change in schedule should be the same regardless of whether the worker's separation *over the issue of schedule* is voluntary or involuntary. It is clearly difficult to distinguish quits from layoffs generally (McLaughlin 1991); and it is especially difficult to attribute the entire cause for a separation to scheduling problems. Scheduling is only one of the many reasons that might induce workers to seek to leave their jobs; and the deterioration of schedule matches between workers and firms is almost certainly one of the more minor reasons that workers are laid off from their jobs. Nonetheless, if a shock to preferences induces the switch, we should expect that voluntary job-changers will exhibit larger differences, $\Delta\sigma^2(\mathrm{d}\ln D)$ and $\Delta\sigma^2(\mathrm{d}\ln H)$, than workers who separated involuntarily.[2] Moreover, differences between quitters and others in the estimates of $\Delta^2 S$ will give a better indication of whether days, or daily hours, are less easily changed within jobs.

The caveat throughout all this discussion is the assumption that wages cannot readily be changed in response to changes in workers' preferences for scheduled days or daily hours. While we know that hourly wages do respond slightly to variations in desired annual hours (Biddle and Zarkin 1989), we know absolutely nothing about whether they respond differently to changes in preferences for days versus daily hours. As long as the responses of wages to changes in D and H are equally weak (or strong), however, $\Delta^2 S$ will provide an unbiased estimate of the relative ease of altering days and daily hours within jobs.

Constructing the Appropriate Data for Analyzing Changing Days and Hours

To make the comparisons implicit in (4.3) we need to obtain panel information on workers' days and daily hours. A reasonable number of the workers in the sample should have changed jobs between the times when they are observed if the data are to provide statistically valid comparisons between stayers and movers. In 1992 (Wave 9), as in 1990 (Wave 7), the GSOEP obtained information from respondents on days and daily hours using the same questions, "How many days per week do you usually work?" and, "How many hours do you usually work per day?" As in the 1990 data this information was only obtained from persons who stated that they worked regular days (or regular hours per day). Also as in the 1990 data, the questions probably refer to workdays and daily hours on the respondent's main job.

To take advantage of this requestioning in the GSOEP, I followed all respondents in the West German sample from 1990 through 1992 and constructed a data set containing information on their job histories over this period. Attrition from the sample over the two years was 14 percent. Of the 7,973 continuing respondents, 3,049 worked regular days and hours in both years and form the basis for calculating $\Delta^2 S$. To distinguish job-stayers from job-changers, I compared the worker's report of job tenure (in months) in 1992 to the difference in months between the dates of the 1990 and 1992 interviews. Those whose 1992 job tenure was less than the elapsed time between interviews (in general, less than two years) were assumed to have changed jobs. This method classified 15 percent of those holding jobs with regular schedules in both years as having switched jobs over this two-year period. The GSOEP also provides information on the reason for job-switching. I thus used information from the 1991 and 1992 interviewing waves to classify job-changers by whether their separation from the 1990 job was voluntary or involuntary. The same two sets of interviews provided data on whether the worker's marital status or other household status (other family members in the respondent's household) changed during this two-year period.

The task of constructing the required sample of panel data for the United States is more difficult, as there are no readily available panel data on a large group of workers' days and daily hours.[3] Because the May CPS Supplements did not contain information on schedules in years adjacent to 1991, linking responses by workers in half the CPS rotation groups in 1991 to their responses in 1990 (for workers in groups 5 through 8) or in 1992 (for workers in groups 1 through 4) is of no use. The most recent pair of adjacent years in which information on schedules was obtained in the May Supplement is 1977 and 1978. Accordingly, I construct a sample of panel data containing information on job schedules by matching people in rotation groups 1 through 4 from the May 1977 CPS to those in rotation groups 5 through 8 from the May 1978 CPS.

The matching process is by no means automatic, as the basic unit of observation in the Current Population Survey is the household location, not the particular family that resides there. I disqualified matches to the May 1978 CPS if the worker failed to match exactly on age (plus one year), race, or gender; if the reported difference in educational attainment between 1978 and 1977 was negative, or was more than 2 years; and (except for Vietnam-era veterans) if the worker's veteran status in 1978 differed from that in 1977.[4] This procedure justified matches for 68 percent of the adults in the first four rotation groups in the May 1977 CPS. As one would expect where failures to match arise chiefly from respondents having moved, successful matches were somewhat older, more likely to be women, and less likely to be Hispanic, black, or other races than in the complete May 1977 sample.[5]

The record for each of the successful matches contains all the information on which the analyses in chapters 2 and 3 were based, including for both 1977 and 1978 scheduled days and daily hours, starting/ending times on the main job, and the usual demographic information in the CPS. Information on schedules was not obtained for self-employed workers in the May CPS Supplements in the 1970s. Thus I base the analyses for both the United States and Germany in the next section solely on the data describing employees.

Another difficulty is that, unlike the data from May 1991 used in chapter 2, the May 1977 and May 1978 CPS Supplements provide information only on scheduled *weekly* hours, DH, not on daily hours. Information about scheduled days of work (the same question we used in chapter 2) is included in these data. One approach would simply divide reported scheduled weekly hours by reported usual days of work; but the division would accentuate any errors in reporting either D or DH.[6] The alternative approach that I adopt is to make assumptions about the correlation between $dlnD$ and the unobserved $dlnH$, call it ρ, to generate a measure of $\sigma^2(dlnH)$ based on the relationship among the variances of the percentage changes in days, daily hours and weekly hours.[7] The calculations based on equations (4.1)-(4.3) thus correspond to the derivation in the previous section and are comparable to the calculations for Germany. All the other analyses of changes in schedules for the United States, including regressions describing the determinants of those changes, use the reported scheduled *weekly* hours.

An equally serious difficulty is that the CPS does not directly identify job-changers. To solve this problem I assume that a worker changed jobs during the 12 months between the surveys if the three-digit industry that he or she listed in May 1978 differed from what was listed in May 1977. This counts as job-stayers those workers who switched firms within a narrowly defined industry, and as job-changers those who transferred within a company to a plant classified in another industry. The net effect of these problems in classification is unclear, but it is likely to be quite small.[8] Also, and probably more important, some workers classified as job-changers may simply have misreported their industrial affiliation in one or both of the samples. The extent of this measurement error cannot be known, but it surely works to reduce $\Delta\sigma^2(dlnD)$ and $\Delta\sigma^2(dlnH)$. So long as rates of intraindustry job-changing and the misreporting of industrial affiliation are not correlated differently with changing days and changing hours, the estimate of $\Delta^2 S$ will be biased toward zero, but its sign will still be correct.

The Ease of Changing Days and Daily Hours

In this section I examine the variances in changes in days and daily hours among workers included in the German and American panel data sets. In addition to estimating $\Delta^2 S$, I also provide checks on those calculations by studying changes in the distributions of the integer measures of days and hours and examine their correlates. Finally, since for some workers there is information on days and hours for one year but not the other, we can study patterns of switching between regular and variable daily schedules and can consider how daily schedules vary with the closeness of attachment to the labor force.

Tables 4.1 present the measures $\sigma^2(\mathrm{dln}D)$ and $\sigma^2(\mathrm{dln}DH)$ for job-stayers and job-changers, based directly on the respondents' answers in the two countries' panel data sets.[9] Table 4.1G also presents calculations of $\sigma^2(\mathrm{dln}H)$ based directly on the answers in the GSOEP and lists the calculations of $\Delta^2 S$ computed from the $\sigma^2(\mathrm{dln}D)$ and $\sigma^2(\mathrm{dln}H)$. The reader should be reminded of the admonition in chapter 2 that reported weekly hours in the GSOEP are not simply workdays times daily hours, but are instead a response to a separate, third question in the survey.

Table 4.1U   Variance in Percentage Changes in Days, Weekly Hours and Daily Hours, 1977-78

	DAYS	WEEKLY HOURS	DAILY HOURS			N
	$\sigma^2(\mathrm{dln}D)$	$\sigma^2(\mathrm{dln}DH)$	$\sigma^2(\mathrm{dln}H)$ Based on			
				$\rho =$		
			0	0.19	0.50	
			Men			
Same industry	0.0188	0.0560	0.0372	0.0284	0.0185	6095
New industry	0.0709	0.1806	0.1097	0.0808	0.0500	2288
		$\Delta^2 S =$	−0.0204	−0.0003	0.0206	
			Women			
Same industry	0.0364	0.0767	0.0403	0.0281	0.0161	4554
New industry	0.1361	0.2889	0.1530	0.1069	0.0614	1407
		$\Delta^2 S =$	−0.0130	0.0209	0.0544	

In constructing table 4.1U, I approximate the variances of daily hours from the respondents' days worked and weekly hours by making assumptions about ρ, the correlation between percentage changes in days and daily hours. Obviously there is no prior information on ρ in the American data. I thus compute the $\sigma^2(\mathrm{dln}H)$ for the United States by simulating using three values of this parameter: (1) $\rho = 0$, not far from the value +0.03 that we find for this parameter in the sample of German stayers; (2) $\rho = +0.19$, the value for the sample of German movers; and (3) $\rho = +0.50$, a very high value of the parameter, probably far outside what one would observe for any sample of continuing workers in an industrialized economy.[10] The values of $\Delta^2 S$ in table 4.1U are listed based on comparing $\sigma^2(\mathrm{dln}D)$ to each calculated value of $\sigma^2(\mathrm{dln}H)$.

Table 4.1G   Variance in Percentage Changes in Days, Daily Hours and Weekly Hours, 1990–92

	DAYS	DAILY HOURS	WEEKLY HOURS		
	$\sigma^2(\mathrm{dln}D)$	$\sigma^2(\mathrm{dln}H)$	$\Delta^2 S$	$\sigma^2(\mathrm{dln}DH)$	N
			Men		
Same job	0.0040	0.0226		.1643	1620
New job:					
All	0.0208	0.0164	.0229	.1486	268
Voluntary	0.0243	0.0187	.0242	.1633	138
Involuntary	0.0165	0.0137	.0214	.1327	130
			Women		
Same job	0.0209	0.0665		.3611	967
New job:					
All	0.0742	0.1593	−.0394	.4815	194
Voluntary	0.0952	0.1519	−.0109	.3878	124
Involuntary	0.0376	0.1714	−.0881	.6502	70

With the exception of daily hours among men in the German sample, the variance of changes in workdays and daily hours is greater among job-changers than among stayers. This is consistent with the simple theoretical idea in the previous section that there are costs of departing from the firm's optimal schedule and that these exceed any cost savings that might be obtained through wage flexibility as schedules are altered. The differences in variances between stayers and changers are quite substantial, suggesting the potential role of altering one's daily schedule as an impetus toward job mobility.

The evidence on the relative sizes of the variances in days and daily hours is mixed. Among German women, German male job-stayers and American men (unless one makes an extreme assumption about ρ) there is more variation in each category in hours than in days. Among American women, however, the variances are roughly equal at reasonable values of this correlation coefficient; and among German male job-changers the variance in days exceeds that in daily hours. While we saw in chapter 2 that there is generally more dispersion in scheduled daily hours than in scheduled days in both countries, that cross-sectional conclusion is only partly supported by longitudinal evidence.

One result from chapter 2 that is strongly supported by this evidence on changes in schedules is the implied greater flexibility of the U.S. labor market along the dimension of days worked. In every category the variances in changes in days, the only dimension on which the data are strictly comparable, are greater in table 4.1U than in table 4.1G. Along the other dimensions the differences between the two countries are mixed. One should remember, however, that changes in schedules in the American data are calculated only over a twelve-month period, while in the German data we are observing changes over a two-year period, so that comparable German data would generate substantially lower variances. The results suggest that it is not just that the U.S. labor market offers a wider range of choices of days on which to work; it also offers people more chance to alter their work schedules, either within the current job or on another to which they can move.

As in Altonji and Paxson (1986; 1992), the results here for the United States suggest that job-changers seek to alter their total hours and find this difficult to do on their current jobs. The results show that this difficulty occurs along both dimensions of their work schedules, workdays and daily hours. Some care is required in making the comparison to Germany here, since weekly hours in the German data are based on responses to a separate question, and are not calculated as days times daily hours.[11] Nonetheless, the results for Germany suggest a strikingly different scenario from what we observe for the United

States: as the equality of the variances for job-stayers and job-changers implies, job-changers, especially men, are not interested in changing their total hours per week. Rather, at least among German men, the results suggest that the main desire is to change the number of days at work, and that this cannot be accomplished within the current job.

One interpretation of the surprising lack of any consistent differences between voluntary and involuntary movers in the German data is that the theory sketched before has some problems, since it applied to demographic shocks that induced workers to seek to alter their schedules. Another is that the distinction between voluntary and involuntary mobility is not important in the context of separations arising from workers' desires for changing schedules, so that we should not expect these measures to differ. A final possibility, consistent with the preceding discussion and with the results for Germany in chapter 2, is that the failure to find differences between voluntary and involuntary movers merely reflects the narrow range of schedules available throughout the German labor market.

The major focus of this section is on $\Delta^2 S$, the "difference-in-difference" of the variances of days and daily hours between movers and stayers. This is the measure that we identified as giving the best estimate of the relative ease of changing days versus changing hours on the current job. The evidence on this issue is mixed. Among German men $\Delta^2 S > 0$, suggesting a greater need to switch jobs to alter days than to alter hours. The exact opposite finding is produced for German women: for them job-switching is motivated more by an urge to alter hours than days. Assuming that the true value of the correlation between days and daily hours in the United States is between 0 and +0.19, the estimates of $\Delta^2 S$ in table 4.1U imply that it is roughly equally easy to alter days and daily hours. That conclusion is strengthened when one notes how small $\Delta^2 S$ is compared to the underlying variances that it comprises, especially the variances in daily hours.

Because of the nature of the data we cannot look at changes in workers' schedules on all their jobs, only their schedules on their main jobs. Nonetheless, this data problem is quite unimportant: if we disqualify those (roughly 7 percent of workers) who had any second job (not merely a long second job) in the first of the two years that we analyze, tables 4.1 change only slightly.[12] The typical worker's behavior is characterized well by the calculations in these tables.

One wonders whether this entire discussion might not be an artifact of treating what are integer measures of days and hours as if they were continuous. Is the apparently small relative difference in the ease of changing days and hours still evident if, instead of calculating the variances of percentage (logarithmic) changes, we examine absolute changes in days and hours among stayers and leavers? Tables 4.2 show the distributions of changes in days and hours (daily hours in Germany, weekly hours in the United States) by gender and for stayers and movers. For both countries it is quite clear that the dispersion of changes is much greater among movers than among stayers. Also reflecting the results in tables 4.1, the relatively greater dispersion among movers than stayers seems about the same for changes in days and changes in hours. The tables provide the one additional piece of information that these differences between movers and stayers occur both among those workers who cut their days and those who increase them, and among those workers who cut their daily hours and those who increase them. There is no evidence of any asymmetry in these data.

Table 4.2U   Changes in Days and Weekly Hours, 1977-78 (Percent Distributions)

	Industry		Industry	
	Same	**New in 1978**	**Same**	**New in 1978**
	DAYS			
Change:				
	Men		Women	
≤ −2	1.23	3.54	2.33	4.69
−1.5 - −1.0	5.50	7.73	4.96	7.82
−0.5 - +0.5	86.40	75.04	85.57	67.72
+1.0 - +1.5	5.47	8.44	4.90	9.24
≥ +2	1.41	5.24	2.24	10.52
	WEEKLY HOURS			
	Men		Women	
≤ −10	6.56	10.97	5.03	9.10
−9 - −3	10.39	9.44	9.20	10.59
−2 - +2	66.54	53.67	70.14	49.39
+3 - +9	9.73	11.23	9.85	11.87
≥ +10	6.68	14.69	5.78	19.05
N =	6095	2288	4554	1407

The general conclusion from this analysis is that employers cannot alter work schedules—days and daily hours—sufficiently to respond to shocks to workers' preferences or family situations. That inability, however, seems to be the same along both of these dimensions of scheduling. The evidence does not suggest that it is any easier for employers to respond to shocks by changing daily hours than by changing days per week.

Table 4.2G   Changes in Days and Daily Hours, 1990-92
(Percent Distributions)

	Industry		Industry	
	Same	**New in 1992**	**Same**	**New in 1992**
		DAYS		
Change:				
		Men		Women
≤-2	0.37	1.87	1.86	4.64
−1	3.02	3.73	3.52	8.25
0	91.73	85.82	89.25	73.71
+1	4.26	7.84	4.14	8.25
≥+2	0.62	0.74	1.24	5.15
		DAILY HOURS		
		Men		Women
≤ -2	2.53	4.10	4.76	8.76
−1.9 – −0.5	17.52	20.15	16.96	18.66
−0.4 – +0.4	54.20	42.17	55.63	37.11
+0.5 – +1.9	20.55	23.51	18.20	20.11
≥ +2	4.20	10.07	4.45	15.46
N =	1620	268	967	194

While information on the magnitudes of changes in days and daily hours is interesting and provides the basic measure of the relative difficulties of changing these aspects of work schedules within a workplace, it does not tell us how these changes relate to the shocks that we viewed as motivating them. In particular, what characteristics of workers make it easier for them to change days and hours without changing jobs? How do changes in days and hours differ in response to life events? Tables 4.3 examine these issues by presenting regressions of

Table 4.3U Least-Squares Estimates of Determinants of Changes in Days and Weekly Hours, 1977–78

	Men		Women	
	|ΔDAYS|	|ΔWEEKLY HOURS|	|ΔDAYS|	|ΔWEEKLY HOURS|
Variable				
Change in marital status	0.016	0.185	–0.049	0.284
	(0.051)	(0.661)	(0.063)	(0.602)
Education	–0.0043	0.0886	–0.0122	0.0652
	(0.0024)	(0.0314)	(0.0039)	(0.0375)
Age	–0.0467	-0.3231	–0.0343	-0.2280
	(0.003)	(0.043)	(0.005)	(0.044)
Age^2/100	0.0517	0.3610	0.0360	0.2483
	(0.004)	(0.051)	(0.006)	(0.053)
New job	1.116	13.143	0.703	7.229
	(0.118)	(1.519)	(0.177)	(1.679)
New job x change in marital status	–0.178	–0.582	0.152	0.587
	(0.088)	(1.131)	(0.100)	(0.954)
New job x education	0.0046	-0.0431	0.0075	0.0626
	(0.0051)	(0.0652)	(0.0089)	(0.0845)
New job x age	–0.0517	–0.5103	–0.0224	–0.2041
	(0.006)	(0.079)	(0.009)	(0.083)
New job x age^2/100	0.0576	0.5566	0.0199	0.1636
	(0.008)	(0.099)	(0.011)	(0.105)
$\overline{R}^2$	.106	.062	.084	.023
p-values (tests of χ^2 statistics describing interactions)				
New job	.00003	.00001	.00001	.00001
N =	8383		5961	

Table 4.3G Least-Squares Estimates of Determinants of Changes in Days and Daily Hours, 1990-92

	Men		Women	
	|ΔDAYS|	|ΔWEEKLY HOURS|	|ΔDAYS|	|ΔWEEKLY HOURS|
Variable				
Change in marital status	0.015	0.035	–0.027	–0.209
	(0.045)	(0.074)	(0.062)	(0.130)
Change in other family at home	–0.0558	0.0348	–0.0355	0.1129
	(0.023)	(0.052)	(0.052)	(0.109)
Education	–0.0046	0.0103	0.0045	0.0330
	(0.004)	(0.009)	(0.010)	(0.020)
Age	–0.0012	0.0026	–0.0009	–0.0068
	(0.0008)	(0.0018)	(0.0017)	(0.0036)
New job	–0.0746	–0.246	0.904	1.008
	(0.162)	(0.363)	(0.470)	(0.981)
New job x change in marital status	–0.178	–0.038	0.131	0.269
	(0.084)	(0.187)	(0.182)	(0.378)
New job x change in children	0.2755	-0.0370	–0.0791	–1.225
	(0.087)	(0.193)	(0.270)	(0.565)
New job x education	0.0281	0.0238	–0.0586	–0.1557
	(0.014)	(0.032)	(0.042)	(0.088)
New job x age	–0.0057	0.0073	–0.0037	0.0420
	(0.0029)	(0.0065)	(0.006)	(0.012)
Quit	0.092	0.376	–0.063	–0.551
	(0.102)	(0.473)	(0.546)	(1.141)
Quit x change in marital status	0.188	0.347	0.047	–0.152
	(0.102)	(0.227)	(0.186)	(0.388)

Table 4.3G (continued)

	Men		Women	
	|ΔDAYS|	|ΔDAILY HOURS|	|ΔDAYS|	|ΔDAILY HOURS|
Quit x other family change	–0.166	-0.129	0.5115	2.375
	(0.102)	(0.227)	(0.346)	(0.723)
Quit x education	–0.0357	–0.0620	0.0001	0.0545
	(0.019)	(0.041)	(0.047)	(0.099)
Quit x age	0.0097	0.0354	0.0065	0.0001
	(0.0046)	(0.074)	(0.007)	(0.015)
$\overline{R}^2$	.016	.017	.035	.059
p-values (tests of χ^2 statistics describing interactions)				
New job	.0003	.589	.500	.002
Quit	.018	.254	.545	.022
New job and quit	.004	.137	.179	.000
N =	1888		1161	

the absolute values of changes in days and hours (daily in Germany, weekly in the United States) as functions of age, education, and changes in marital status and in the presence of other family members (usually children). To infer how these characteristics and life events are related to the ease of changing schedules within jobs, they are interacted with a dummy variable for workers who obtained a new job. To distinguish these effects further, in the regressions based on German data I also include interactions with a dummy variable measuring whether the worker quit or changed jobs for other reasons.

The first thing to note in the tables is that the vectors of interactions of the variables measuring demographic changes and workers' characteristics with new-job status are generally significant. Indeed, even the distinction between voluntary and involuntary job changes in the German data is useful for examining how these factors affect work schedules. It is not just that these characteristics are related to changes in schedules, although they are. Rather, they are related to schedule changes that are effected through job changes.

This relationship exists for changes in marital and other family status in some of the regressions, but only weakly so for educational attainment. By far the biggest effect is in the interaction with age, an effect that is strikingly clear in the U.S. data.[13] Schedule changes show a U- shaped relation with age. Workers who do not change jobs seem to settle down to a schedule that suits them up to a point roughly in their late forties, at which age their days and hours start changing more rapidly. These changes that relate to age cannot be fully accommodated within most workplaces, as the interactions show that schedules of those who change jobs exhibit a similar life cycle. This longitudinal evidence is quite consistent with the evidence in table 2.5U of a very clear and strong inverse U-shaped life cycle in work schedules, with both days and hours peaking in the late middle of workers' careers. The results here essentially demonstrate how cross-section differences translate into changes over the life cycle that naturally have signs opposite their cross-section counterparts.[14]

All of the discussion thus far has dealt with workers who are employed over the one- or two- year (in the German data) intervals that we examine. Additional light on the determination of days and hours can be obtained by comparing these workers to others who are employed in only one of the two years (in the German data, also including workers who do not have regular schedules in both years). Consider first table 4.4U, which shows for 1977 (1978) a comparison of days worked by continuing job-holders and those who were not employed in 1978 (1977). Simple χ^2 tests show that these distributions are very strongly significantly different from each other. Continuing job-holders are much more likely to be working regular five-day weeks than workers who are employed in only one of the two years. This is not merely because workers who are less closely attached to the labor force work fewer days when they are employed: there are also more people with very many days per week among those who are not employed in one of the two years. Apparently the American labor market's need for workers with unusual weekly schedules, *both long and short schedules in terms of days worked,* is met disproportionately by recruiting people with a high probability of nonemployment.

Just as the U.S. data allow us to infer the relation between attachment to employment and work schedules, the German data allow us to infer the extent of persistence of irregular schedules. Table 4.5G presents a transition matrix of probabilities of movement between irregular and regular job schedules (days and hours). The evidence it provides is striking: the majority of German workers who are employed in two consecutive years and who were working on irregular schedules (days or hours) in the first year are working on regular schedules in the second. Irregular schedules in Germany appear to be quite transient states for the majority of workers on them. While the American data do not permit examining this phenomenon, the generally greater fluidity and flexibility of the U.S. labor market suggest at least as strong an inference would be drawn if such data were available.

The results in tables 4.4U and 4.5G are strong evidence that workers' preferences underlie the behavior that has been documented in this section. It is very difficult to argue that somehow the menu of choices that employers offer workers changes from one year to the next. On the other hand, it is quite reasonable to argue that changes in workers' desires for certain kinds of schedules cause them to change jobs or leave employment when the technology of scheduling on their old job makes it costly for their employers to accommodate their changed preferences or circumstances.

Table 4.4U   Scheduled Days of Continuing Workers, Labor Force Entrants and Exits (Percent Distributions)

| | 1977 | | 1978 | |
	Both years	Exits	Both years	Entrants
		Men		
Days				
1	0.63	2.98	0.33	2.58
2	0.98	3.76	0.91	4.42
3	2.09	4.54	1.67	6.08
4	2.42	4.28	2.39	6.35
4.5	0.36	0.26	0.29	0.28
5	74.45	64.36	75.90	59.30
5.5	4.66	4.67	4.80	5.80
6	11.86	12.31	11.21	11.97
7	2.55	2.85	2.51	3.22
N =	8383	1543	8343	1086
		Women		
Days				
1	1.76	5.17	1.39	6.24
2	3.24	7.45	2.75	7.68
3	5.72	7.64	5.07	11.19
4	5.59	7.51	5.33	7.82
4.5	0.72	0.74	0.84	0.72
5	76.33	62.93	78.33	58.61
5.5	1.44	1.17	1.48	1.36
6	4.18	5.85	4.13	4.66
7	1.02	1.54	0.69	1.72
N =	5961	1624	8343	1394

Table 4.5G   Changing Regularity of Days and Daily Hours, 1990 to 1992

	Men		Women	
Probability of moving from:		N		N
Variable to fixed days	0.540	113	0.798	94
Fixed to variable days	0.032	2200	0.036	1470
Irregular to regular hours	0.690	190	0.661	124
Regular to irregular hours	0.072	2123	0.059	1346

The Dynamics of Nonstandard Work Times

In this section I examine how workers' daily schedules change from one year to the next. Unfortunately this examination can be conducted only on the American data, as the GSOEP obtained no information on daily schedules in 1992.[15] Thus unlike the analyses in the earlier chapters of this monograph, no comparative research is offered. The U.S. data are again from the match of the May 1977 and 1978 Current Population Surveys.

Unlike the May 1991 CPS, the CPS Supplements from the 1970s did not always list daily schedules on both the main and any second jobs. As the evidence in chapter 3 showed, however, the paucity of people holding long second jobs means that little is lost when the analysis is restricted to primary jobs alone. A bigger difficulty is that, as I noted in section 4.2, not all of the respondents in the two CPS Supplements could be matched. Among those who could, demographic events between May 1977 and May 1978, such as marriage or divorce, are fairly uncommon. Coupling these facts with the evidence from table 3.2U that work at evenings or nights is performed by no more than 20 percent of employees means that it is difficult to use the data to discover how changing demographic circumstances generate changes in daily schedules. Instead, all we can discover is whether work at different times of the day is performed by the same or rotating groups of people, and how workers' characteristics are related to their likelihood of staying with unusual work schedules. In other words, the discussion below complements chapter 3 by examining flows into and out of different daily schedules.

Consider first figure 4.1U, which is based solely on people who worked in both May 1977 and May 1978. For each hour of the day, and separately for workers who remained on the same job (really, in the same narrowly defined industry) or changed jobs, it shows what percentage of these workers were at work in both years compared to the number who were at work at that hour on average during the two years.[16] Remember from figure 3.1U that in May 1991 roughly 85 percent of all workers were at work between 9AM and 3PM. Figure 4.1U demonstrates that work schedules that involve these hours are fairly stable: someone at work between 9AM and 3PM during 1977 who stayed on the same job had a 95 percent chance of working at that time in 1978. The implications for work at nonstandard times, such as evenings or nights, are much different. The figure shows that little more than half of the workers who worked at unusual times in 1977 and remained with the same job in 1978 worked at unusual times in the second year.

Figure 4.1U   Fraction of Continuing Workers at Work in Both 1977 and 1978

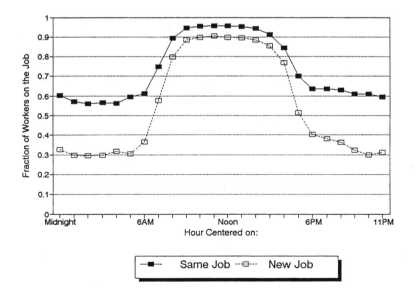

The conclusions are even stronger for workers who changed jobs between 1977 and 1978. Most job-changers who worked at standard times in 1977 changed to jobs that kept them working at those standard times; but roughly only one-third of job-changers who were working at unusual times in 1977 were at work at those times in 1978. At each hour of the day job-changers are twice as likely to change their daily schedules as job-stayers. The difference between movers and stayers underscores the results in the previous section that job-changing is a major route by which workers shift out of schedules that no longer accord with their preferences and the incentives that they face.

Table 4.6U, based on transition matrices describing work at unusual times in the two years, recasts the results implicit in figure 4.1U and also disaggregates by gender. Among other things it shows the percentage of job-stayers who worked evenings in 1977 who continued to do so in 1978 (among men, 61.76 percent). As another example, it illustrates the percentage of job-stayers who did not work evenings in 1977 but who did so in 1978 (among men, 7.70 percent). Job-changers are quite unlikely to stick with schedules that require work in evenings or at night, but more likely than job-stayers to move into such work. Both probabilities are higher among women workers than their male counterparts. Job-stayers switch away from evening and night work at fairly high rates; and the probability of moving into such work is fairly low among stayers. Here, however, the chances of moving into or out of this work are higher among men than among women.

The general picture is that evening or night work is something that continuing labor force participants do not do for very long stretches of time. Work at nonstandard times appears to be quite fluid: each year nearly half of regular workers leave such schedules for work at more standard times.[17] This fluidity seems to accord with the cross-section results of chapter 3 on the inferiority of work at unusual times.

Finding such fluidity of work at unusual times among continuing workers leads to the question of whether workers who are less attached to the labor force are more or less likely to be working at these times. To answer this we can compare work schedules among the continuing participants whose behavior underlies figure 4.1U and table 4.6U to those among people who left employment between May 1977 and May 1978, and those among previously nonemployed workers who found jobs during this period. The comparisons are presented in table 4.7U.

Working evenings or nights in both 1977 and 1978 was more common among people who entered or left employment during the intervening twelve months than among those who remained employed. Work at nonstandard times is especially the province of people who are new to the labor force, or at least new to employment. The differences are more pronounced among women, with the rate of work at nonstandard times nearly 50 percent higher among labor force entrants and exits than among women who remained employed over this period.

Table 4.6U   Probability of Nonstandard Work Time in 1978 in Relation to 1977 Work Schedule, Continuing Workers (Percentages)

	Industry		**Industry**	
	Same	**New in 1978**	**Same**	**New in 1978**
	Working 7PM – 10PM May 1978			
	Men		Women	
Working 7PM – 10PM May 1977:				
No	7.70	11.62	4.85	12.45
Yes	61.76	38.01	60.76	31.43
	Working 10PM – 6AM May 1978			
	Men		Women	
Working 10PM – 6AM May 1977:				
No	6.45	10.13	4.76	10.26
Yes	69.57	38.18	64.44	30.00
N =	5505	2053	4123	1281

In chapter 3 and for continuing workers we found that the likelihood of working at unusual times is highest among those who have the least amount of human capital. The results for entrants and exits presented in table 4.7U suggest that the same conclusion applies for those unobserved characteristics that indicate that workers are less stable. It is difficult to explain these outcomes by pointing to the effects of employers' behavior, but quite easy to rationalize them as the result of workers acquiring seniority and moving out of jobs with schedules that they generally view as unattractive.

Table 4.7U   Percentage of Workers with Nonstandard Work Times Among Continuing Workers and Labor Force Entrants and Exits

	1977		1978	
	Both years	Exits	Both years	Entrants
	Men			
At Work:				
7PM – 10PM	18.23	22.83	17.19	22.80
10PM – 6AM	16.05	16.27	16.21	18.39
N =	7558	1708	7558	1430
	Women			
At Work:				
7PM – 10PM	14.77	21.01	13.23	22.57
10PM – 6AM	12.75	16.27	12.34	17.46
N =	5404	1709	5404	1564

Tables 3.3 showed that additional years of schooling reduce the likelihood that someone will be working evenings or nights, and that in the United States, though not in Germany, there is a U-shaped relationship between age and the probability of work at these times. I interpreted these relationships as reflecting choices to avoid such work by people with more human capital. But is that correct; or do the correlations merely reflect the behavior of firms that promote continuing workers into jobs that have more standard work schedules?

To examine these possibilities I estimate equations describing the probability of working in the evening or at night among people who were not employed in May 1977 but were in May 1978. Because the equations are estimated using ordinary least squares, each coefficient shows the change in the probability of such work.[18] Table 4.8U presents these results. Note first that, although the $\bar{R}^2$ seem low, they are no different from those describing the cross-section results in tables 3.3U. Clearly, as noted in chapter 3, there is substantial individual variation in the probability of working at unusual times.

For the schooling and the age variables the similarities to the results in tables 3.3U are striking: the negative impact of an additional year of schooling on the probability of evening or night work is roughly the same among those who enter the workforce as it is in the cross-section results in chapter 3. The same U-shaped relationship to age also exists among these job entrants, with the lowest probability again being reached shortly before age 50. Here, however, the declines in the probabilities before that age and the rises afterward are much sharper than among all workers. That strengthens the interpretation of the relationship as stemming from people using their human capital (and the higher full income it generates) to "buy" more desirable schedules, since especially in this group very junior and very senior workers are likely to have relatively low skills compared to more regular workers of the same age.

Table 4.8U   Least-Squares Estimates of Coefficients in the Determinants of the Probability of Working at Nonstandard Times in 1978,   Main Job, Labor Force Entrants

	Men		Women	
	Probability Working in 1978:			
	7PM – 10PM	**10PM – 6AM**	**7PM – 10PM**	**10PM – 6AM**
Probability:	.228	.184	.226	.175
Variable				
Years of schooling	–.0076	–.0134	–.0081	–.0015
	(.0038)	(.0036)	(.0044)	(.0040)
Age	–.0272	–.0097	–.0229	–.0136
	(.0046)	(.0043)	(.0046)	(.0043)
Age^2/100	.0294	.0106	.0241	.0162
	(.0054)	(.0050)	(.0056)	(.0052)
Married 1977	–.0847	–.0745	–.0548	–.0469
	(.0652)	(.0612)	(.0467)	(.0432)
Married 1978	.1111	.1196	.0512	.0592
	(.0642)	(.0603)	(.0455)	(.0421)
Black	–.0013	.0552	–.0291	.0306
	(.0405)	(.0380)	(.0347)	(.0321)
Hispanic	.0102	–.0270	–.0007	.0553
	(.0503)	(.0472)	(.0500)	(.0463)
$\overline{R}^2$	.047	.016	.044	.008
N =	1430		1564	

In the cross-section analysis of chapter 3, married men and women were significantly less likely than others to be working evenings and nights. Among these new entrants there is little difference between those who are married in both 1977 and 1978 and those who are single in both years. (The effect of being continuously married is the sum of the coefficients on marital status in both years.) What is interesting is the effect of changing marital status: people who were unmarried in 1977 but married in 1978 were much more likely (though not highly significantly so) to be working evenings or nights if they entered work during this period, while those who became single during these twelve months were less likely to enter evening or night work. In the cross section among all workers, we saw in chapter 3 that blacks are significantly more likely to work nonstandard times than whites, while Hispanics generally tend to differ little from non-Hispanic whites. The evidence in Table 4.8U shows that among labor force entrants there again is no evidence of any difference between Hispanics and non-Hispanic whites; and only for night work is there even a hint of the much higher incidence of work at unusual times by black workers.

Conclusions and Implications

This chapter has gone beyond its predecessors by offering analyses of how people's work schedules change over time. The main gains from this approach result from its allowing us to abstract from unobservable individual-specific effects in order to analyze how changing events affect schedules. Among the major findings are the following.

Workers change days and daily hours in both countries mostly by switching jobs.

It is easier to change days and daily hours without changing jobs in the United States than in Germany, suggesting yet another dimension along which the U.S. labor market is relatively more flexible.

Employers do not generally find it easier to change daily hours than to change days in response to workers' desires for a change in schedules.

Working irregular days and hours in Germany, or in the evening or at night in the United States, is disproportionately done by workers who are newly employed. Only half of Americans who work evenings or nights in one year will be doing so a year later.

Workers in the United States settle into regular jobs whose daily and weekly schedules are changing little by the time they reach their 40s, but which start to vary more as they near retirement.

Taken together the results in this chapter reinforce the cross-section studies of chapter 3, in that they demonstrate again that lack of human capital is a major correlate of work at nonstandard times. They add, however, the general result that looseness of attachment to the labor force also substantially increases the likelihood of work at these times. Indeed, the most general result of this chapter is that irregular schedules and work at unusual times are incredibly fluid: most workers do not stay on such schedules for very long, so that much of the work at unusual times that we observe is by people who are new to employment and who by inference will soon be moving on to more regular schedules and more standard times of the day.[19] For many workers unusual schedules can be viewed as an unpleasantness that is assigned to newcomers to the workplace.

The evidence in chapters 2 and 3 suggested that low-skilled and minority workers bear yet an additional burden in the labor market, that of working at undesirable times for which wage premiums are insufficient compensation. The findings here should alleviate some of the concern about these differences in work schedules among groups of workers. With the evidence that work at unusual times and on unusual schedules is quite fluid, we can be fairly sure that a large fraction of the total burden imposed by such work is shuffled fairly rapidly among different individuals within the population of lower-skilled workers. If we are concerned about intergroup differences, we should be concerned about the burden of work at unusual times; if we care more about individual differences, the distribution of schedules is a much smaller problem.

NOTES

1. This approach is an extended version of that of Altonji and Paxson (1986; 1992). They examined changes in weekly (or annual) hours among job changers, thus effectively estimating the equivalent of (4.1) or (4.2).

2. This assumes that the distributions of subsequent workdays and daily hours among the two groups of job-leavers are not truncated differently because more workers in one of the groups are unable to find work and thus drop out of our sample.

3. The 1973 and 1977 quality of Employment Surveys provide information on work schedules and permit constructing a longitudinal sample. The difficulty with using them is that the surveys were relatively small, so that the cell sizes would be very tiny, less than half even of the small samples obtainable from the GSOEP.

4. This disqualification rule is excessively stringent, as people's racial identification may change over time. Also, for as much as 2 percent of the sample the respondent's age might differ by 0 or 2 years, because the CPS may be administered at a different time during the week containing May 19.

5. Card (1996) uses a similar, though slightly less conservative, matching procedure to link adjacent annual CPS samples. Starting with males only, he successfully matches 69 percent of the respondents in the first year to observations 12 months later.

6. Indeed, that is exactly what occurs when one makes this calculation. For some workers this gives the absurd result that they are putting in more than 24 hours per day.

7. To see this relationship, note that we can write:

$$\sigma^2(\mathrm{dln}DH) = \sigma^2(\mathrm{dln}H) + 2\rho\{\sigma^2(\mathrm{dln}D)\}^{.5}\{\sigma^2(\mathrm{dln}H)\}^{.5} + \sigma^2(\mathrm{dln}D),$$

which is quadratic equation in $\{\sigma^2(\mathrm{dln}H)\}^{.5}$. Solving this equation yields:

$$\sigma(\mathrm{dln}H) = \{\sigma^2(\mathrm{dln}DH) - [1-\rho^2]\sigma^2(\mathrm{dln}D)\}^{.5} - \rho\sigma(\mathrm{dln}D).$$

8. Some very old evidence (Palmer 1954) suggests that most interindustry mobility is across two-digit SIC industry lines. Evidence from the monthly counts of manufacturing turnover (published by the Bureau of Labor Statistics until 1982) suggests interplant transfers are a minute proportion of total turnover.

9. I could have based the estimates in tables 4.1 on adjusted days and daily hours (using cross-section estimates like those in tables 2.5). This would be analogous to what Altonji and Paxson (1986) did. Given the low $\overline{R}^2$ in those tables, this adjustment would make only minute differences, as it probably also did in their study.

10. Aside from the very strong longitudinal evidence from Germany supporting this assertion, the fairly low cross-section correlations in table 2.3U between days and daily hours in 1991 support the notion that the true value of this parameter is far below .5.

11. The relationship among the variances of days, daily hours and weekly hours implied by the calculations presented in table 4.1G would clearly be impossible if one of these measures were calculated from responses to questions that generated the other two.

12. For example, for men in the United States the variances in the first two rows and columns of table 5.1 change to 0.0190 and 0.0558, 0.0704 and 0.1711. For men in Germany the analogous figures are 0.0042 and 0.0236, 0.0219 and 0.0154. The differences from the tabulated variances are equally small when we exclude workers with a second job in either of the two years.

13. No interactions with Age^2 are included in table 4.3 G, because the quadratic term never had a t-statistic above 0.5.

14. A relationship that has positive linear and negative quadratic terms in the cross-section will have a negative linear term if it is differenced.

15. Shortly before this monograph went to press (in the middle of 1995), the GSOEP collected these data from its respondents, thus allowing future researchers to conduct these analyses for the Germany workforce.

16. The calculation is $E_{t\text{Both}}/[E_{t\text{Both}} + .5[E_{t1977} + E_{t1978}]]$, where t is the particular hour of the day, and the subscript denotes in which year the person worked.

17. If 0.164 is the steady-state fraction of regular male employees working at night, we can use weighted averages of the first two columns in table 4.6U to calculate the flow rates into and out of work at such times. The implied rate of inflow is 0.0623 per year, and the implied rate of outflow is 0.0639 (essentially equal, as one would expect). These imply a renewal rate of nearly 40 percent per annum.

18. Use of the appropriate probit estimator produced results that were qualitatively identical.

19. A similar fluidity in the holding of second jobs in the United States is observed by Paxson and Sicherman (1996).

CHAPTER 5

The Dimensions of Work Time in the Workplace

Thus far I have examined the integrative and instantaneous dimensions of time use mainly from the worker's perspective. While chapters 2 through 4 acknowledged that the outcomes result from the joint determination of schedules by workers (households) and employers, the underlying data described only workers; and the analysis concentrated on the individual. In this chapter I rectify that for integrative time use by analyzing employers' demands for different dimensions of labor.

There has been a substantial amount of theorizing about employers' demands for workers and hours (see the summary by Hart 1987) and also a fair amount of empirical work. In each case, however, as in the study of integrative time use from the perspective of the household, the focus has been on employers' choices between adding extra workers and adding another hour of work *per week* to the assignments of their workers. The distinction between days and daily hours has simply not been paid any attention either in the theory or in the empirical analysis.

The absence of any focus on this topic is rather surprising. There has long been substantial interest in how workers' productivity varies over the working day (for example, Florence 1924 and, most recently, Hamermesh 1990). People sleep and recuperate from work after each *workday*, not after each workweek. Thus, to the extent that workers do tire over a day, rather than only over a week, their productivity may differ along the different margins of work time. Increasing work time by 25 percent by adding 2 hours per day to 8-hour days may have a different effect on output from the same increase in work time produced by adding a fifth day of work per week. The two may generate different costs per worker because of the need to coordinate workers' schedules with the time of the available capital stock (Stafford 1980). Yet another cause is the existence of daily set-up costs, such as security and health checks, that raise the price of days relative to hours. All of these considerations will lead employers who seek to minimize the cost of production to be interested in how long workers are employed each day rather than only in the total number of hours per week.

Even if there are no differences in productivity between days and daily hours on average or at the margin, the imposition of labor market policies makes this distinction important for employers' choices. Consider the laws and institutions governing overtime hours in the United States and Germany. In the United States workers must be paid a 50 percent premium over their regular hourly pay (including premiums for shift work, incentive pay, etc.) on all hours in excess of 40 per week, though in some cases (mainly governmental subunits) compensatory time can be provided in lieu of overtime pay. Note that there is *no daily limit* on hours beyond which the overtime premium must be applied in the United States. The situation is different in Germany. For adults, long-standing legislation limits the regular workday to 10 hours in a workweek limited to 48 hours (Erdmann 1957). The legislative constraint is hardly relevant, as collective and other agreements limit the normal workday to 8 hours or less with a 25 percent premium rate for overtime. Note that in the BRD there are *constraints on both daily and weekly hours*, a crucial difference that means that German employers will have different demands for hours and days than their otherwise identical American counterparts. Also, a cut in the hours at which the overtime premium becomes payable will have different effects in the two countries.

Although related to laws governing overtime, policies governing the length of the workday are somewhat separate and have received much attention (and use, especially in Europe). To answer questions about the impact of such cuts on productivity and about their potential for creating new jobs we need to know more about employers' demands for workers, days, and hours. Similarly, widely heralded attempts to alter the workweek by cutting days (perhaps making the four-day workweek standard) can be analyzed properly only if we have distinguished between the roles of days and hours in production.

The basic question underlying both the policy issues and the general technical problem is the extent to which employers can substitute among workers, days, and daily hours. If employers treat days and daily hours as perfect substitutes, i.e., if there is some method of aggregation that justifies writing weekly hours as the product of days and hours in a production function, making this distinction will not advance upon previous research that merely looks at substitution between employment and weekly hours. Of course, the appropriateness of that aggregation has never been tested, so that at the very least this chapter can validate previous research. If such simple aggregation is not possible, however, then only by examining formally how employers substitute among these three dimensions of labor, as I do in this chapter, can we begin to analyze policies related to hours and days.

What We Know So Far

The central issue noted in the introduction—how employers treat days and daily hours in deciding how to utilize their workers' time—has not been examined at all in the economics literature. The closest approximation has been a small amount of research on the role of shift work in production. As I showed in chapter 3, however, shift work and the timing of work are not closely related, so even this strand of research is only tangentially related to studying employers' choices of days and hours. The leading research in this area is by Betancourt and Clague (1981), who focussed on the relation of shift work to firms' capital-labor ratios. The general result, documented in a variety of sets of data, is that shift work (and, by inference, long workdays for machines, though not necessarily for individual workers) is more prevalent where production is more capital-intensive.

Most research has concentrated on employers' ability to substitute hours for employees and, more generally, on the productivity of workers and hours. An early literature simply estimated Cobb-Douglas-type production functions (usually based on time-series data covering manufacturing or the entire economy) that included both total employment and weekly hours per worker (and sometimes also capital) as inputs into production. (See, for example, Feldstein 1967.) The general result of these studies is that a 1 percent increase in hours per worker seems to add more to output than does a 1 percent increase in employment, though there are not increasing returns to hours of work alone (Hart and McGregor 1988). This often-repeated finding is interesting, though why it should occur is absolutely unclear on theoretical grounds. After all, given equal costs, why do employers fail to keep substituting along the more productive dimension of labor until the productivities of each dimension are equated at the margin?

More recent research has aimed directly at inferring the extent of substitution among workers, hours, and (in some cases also) capital. (A full treatment of this literature is contained in Hamermesh 1993, chapter 3.) One strand, using mostly data on Germany, is particularly noteworthy. Hart and Kawasaki (1988) measure fixed and variable labor costs, implicitly the prices of workers and hours, more carefully than anyone else. They find that the effects of labor cost increases on the demand for both workers and hours are more important than any substitution, and that increasing the relative price of employment or hours increases the relative demand for capital. König and Pohlmeier (1988, 1989) attempt to measure the prices of hours and workers by calculating indexes of overtime premiums and various employee benefits. Theirs are the only available studies that provide direct estimates of worker-hours substitution. They imply that an increase in the price of workers decreases the demand for hours at a fixed output, and that they are jointly substitutes for capital. The results indicate that it may be possible to aggregate workers and hours, but the aggregator is clearly not multiplicative. That is, we cannot write a firm's input of labor L as $L = E[DH]$, where E is employment, D days per week and H hours per day (so that DH is weekly hours).

A second group of studies estimates equations describing firms' demand for employees and hours, focusing on the impact of such changes in policy as raising premium pay for overtime work or cutting standard weekly hours.[1] Studies based on American data compute the demand for employees as a function of the ratio of the cost of (what the authors believe are) per-worker benefits to the wage rate. Along with earlier studies the leading American work, Ehrenberg and Schumann (1982), indicates that employment would rise by perhaps 1 to 2 percent in response to an increase of 1/3 in the price of an hour of overtime (changing the overtime penalty from 50 to 100 percent). It implies that, *at a constant input of workhours*, a higher effective per-hour cost imposed by an increased overtime penalty induces employers to increase the ratio of hours to employees when the cost of an employee rises. One should note that this says nothing about the total effect on employment demand, since the policy raises labor costs and thus induces a negative scale effect on the demand for both hours and workers. This latter effect is underlined by Franz and König (1986), who examine the effects of changing standard weekly hours and raising the overtime penalty using time-series data. The interesting result, consistent with Hart and Kawasaki, is that raising the overtime penalty actually reduces total employment (through the scale effect on the demand for worker-hours).

Research on European and Asian economies has concentrated on examining how mandating lower standard hours would affect weekly hours and total employment.[2] One should note that here too the obvious substitution effect in favor of increased employment could be offset by a negative scale effect as employers cut back the size of their operations and use more capital-intensive techniques when labor becomes more expensive. The results in this literature suggest that cutting weekly hours does create jobs, but that the majority of the cut in hours is not recouped in higher employment.

There is a little evidence that employers treat employees and hours as substitutes in production when their relative prices change, although the extent of substitution is not strong. This means that raising overtime penalties or cutting standard hours will cause an increase in employment *relative* to hours. Similarly, the evidence that extra hours are more productive than extra workers suggests that we should not treat workhours as independent of the dimension of work. We know nothing, however, about how employers substitute among workers, days, and daily hours, since these have not been studied before. As this perusal of the literature should demonstrate, we really know quite little even about the simpler question of how they substitute between workers and weekly hours.

How Employers Choose Among Workers, Days, and Hours

In studying substitution among these dimensions of work time we are really asking a variety of questions. We seek to discover how, given the current configuration of workers, days, and hours, the typical employer will respond to an increase in demand for the product. Ideally we would like to know this both in the short run, when the employer is limited to the existing stock of capital, and the long run, when choices about margins of labor inputs can be combined with choices about the amount of capital. We wish to find out how firms respond to imposed changes in the quantities they may use along these various margins. How do their choices of days, hours, and workers react to imposed limits on days per week (e.g., four days per worker) or hours per day (e.g., 7-1/2 hours)? Finally, we would like to know how they respond to changes in cost at each margin of labor input. That is, how do increases in, for example, the hourly wage rate or the tax rate on wages below some small annual amount (as in the Federal Unemployment Tax that finances unemployment insurance benefits in the United States) affect employers' demands for workers, days, and hours, both relatively and absolutely?

Clearly, we are not going to be able to answer all of these questions in this first investigation of how employers treat days and hours in production. A particularly difficult issue is the last one, employers' responses to changes in relative costs along these different margins of labor input. Though a number of the studies of substitution between employment and weekly hours claim to do so, except for the overtime premium it is very difficult to identify *and measure* costs tied to a particular dimension of labor input. It is not sufficient to compare wage costs (assumed to be per hour and per worker) to benefit costs (assumed to be per worker). For example, a rise in the U.S. payroll tax that finances Social Security retirement and disability benefits (OASDI) increases the cost of both a worker and an additional hour at most wage levels, as does an increase in pension costs in most cases. Health benefits are reasonably assumed to represent per-worker costs, but even here limitations on benefits for part-time workers make the distinction less than clear. Even the studies that make the most progress on this (Hart and Kawasaki 1988; König and Pohlmeier 1989) attribute costs to workers or hours in ways that are debatable.

If these problems arise in dealing with the simpler distinction, employees-weekly hours, they are even more severe in dealing with the threefold categorization of work time as employees, days, and daily hours. In theory there is no problem. We can identify an imposed increase in the hourly wage rate (perhaps as a result of a changed union contract) as raising the cost of all three dimensions proportionately. A Christmas bonus available to all workers regardless of days or hours worked raises the cost of employees only. A particularly intriguing example of demand-side fixed daily costs occurs in the currency-destruction operations of the New York Federal Reserve Bank, where each employee must endure a two-hour security check at the end of the workday. Not surprisingly, the typical worker is on the job four days for ten hours each day.

In practice it is extremely difficult to sort out these distinctions and to obtain data that give a reasonable proxy for differences in relative costs along the three dimensions. In the United States recent establishment-based data offer information only on wages and the presence of pension and health plans. Older establishment data do distinguish among various benefit costs in more detail; but the distinctions are not fine enough to allow inferring which costs might apply to days and which to hours. The situation in other economies may be better, as some of the research summarized in the previous section shows; but even there the data are insufficient for the finer distinction between days and daily hours.

These problems necessitate a different approach, one that avoids the need to identify costs along various margins of labor input. Instead, I rely on inferring directly the relative productivity and ease of substitution between these alternative margins. This method harks back to the literature of the 1960s that was concerned with the relative productivity of workers and hours. It expands upon this, however, by also examining substitution possibilities (and, of course, by considering the three dimensions of labor).

The approach that I use here, which is necessitated both by the logical difficulties (though not impossibilities) of classifying labor costs along each margin and by the complete absence of data on these costs, will do very well at identifying the relative productivities of work time along the three dimensions. Obversely, it is also excellent for inferring how reductions along a particular dimension would have to be met by increases along the others if production is to be maintained. Unfortunately it provides only indirect evidence on the extent to which employers' choices along these dimensions respond to changes in their relative costs. It is thus less useful for analyzing the impacts of changes in overtime penalties, be they of the U.S. or the German variety. In short, this approach is perfectly satisfactory for discussing policies that mandate changes in quantities of labor inputs. It is less useful for studying policies that directly impose changes in their prices.

Inferring Substitution and Productivity along Several Dimensions of Labor

To understand how employers treat the various dimensions of work time I estimate directly the production function that links the several aspects of labor services to output. In general the approach involves estimating the parameters of functions like:

$$(5.1) \quad Y = F(E, D, H) \cdot G(X),$$

or:

$$(5.1') \quad Y = F(E, D, H, K) \cdot G(X),$$

where Y is output, K is the stock of capital, and X is a vector of workers' characteristics that might increase their ability to add to output in the particular unit under consideration. The absence of information on prices of the dimensions of labor services makes direct estimation of some specific form of (5.1) the only feasible approach to inferring substitution among E, D and H (and K), and how their relative productivities differ.

Implicit in specifying (5.1) and (5.1') are a number of assumptions that are usually kept hidden when statistical depictions of the technology underlying the demand for inputs are presented. Most important, once we specify these equations, we implicitly assume that technology confronts each unit of observation (establishments, firms, industries, or entire economies) with the same menu of combinations of the particular inputs, and that differences in the pattern of input prices join with that menu to produce a set of cost-minimizing demands for those inputs. Moreover, each of the underlying decision makers is assumed to treat these prices as parametric, so that we are estimating outcomes generated by the behavior of employers, not by an interaction of their behavior with that of workers. These assumptions are completely standard in the literature and underlie the vast array of estimated production functions and input-demand relationships that have generated our knowledge of the demand for investment goods, labor, and other inputs. They are required in order to make any inferences about the central issues in the study of demand for inputs. They are, however, by no means innocuous.

Including measures of labor quality, X, in these equations accounts for the likelihood that at the same input of workers, days, and daily hours those employees who are better educated and more experienced will be able to produce more. Given our demonstration in chapter 2 that there are separate and distinct life cycles in both days and hours per day, failing to account for the human capital embodied in workers would bias estimates of the effects of differences in inputs of days and hours on output. That variables measuring human capital belong in production functions like (5.1) and (5.1') has been well documented for nearly 30 years, beginning with work by Griliches (1969) and Welch (1970).

The simpler specification of (5.1) is a generalized multifactor Cobb-Douglas production function that just extends the literature of the 1960s to allow for three dimensions of labor time:

$$(5.2) \quad \ln Y = \alpha_0 + \alpha_1 \ln E + \alpha_2 \ln D + \alpha_3 \ln H + g(X),$$

where the α_i are production parameters to be estimated. If we can obtain measures of the stock of capital, the term $\alpha_4 \ln K$ is added to (5.2). This specification does not restrict the production function to have constant returns to scale. It thus allows us to examine whether the increasing returns to hours noted in the 1960s literature are observable when we do not restrict days and daily hours to have the same percentage effects on output.

The difficulty with the specification in (5.2) is that it imposes severe restrictions on the implied responses of employers' demands for workers, days, and hours (and capital services) to changes in their relative costs. In particular, for a fixed level of costs (5.2) restricts the percentage change in the relative productivities of each dimension of labor used in a particular labor market to be equal and opposite the percentage change in the relative amounts of the inputs used in that market. (All partial elasticities of complementarity, c_{ij}, are assumed to be 1.)

These restrictions make the estimates based on (5.2) useless for inferring the effects of policies that impose limits on D or H or that alter their relative costs to employers.

Because of these problems with (5.2), I specify production completely generally using the translog approximation (Christensen, et al. 1973) as:

$$(5.3) \quad \ln Y = \alpha_0 + \alpha_E \ln E + \alpha_D \ln D + \alpha_H \ln H + 0.5\{\beta_{EE}[\ln E]^2 +$$
$$\beta_{DD}[\ln D]^2 + \beta_{HH}[\ln H]^2\} + \beta_{ED}\ln E \ln D + \beta_{EH}\ln E \ln H +$$
$$\beta_{DH}\ln D \ln H + g(X),$$

where as before the α_i are parameters, as are the β_{ij}. If we include a measure of the stock of capital, the terms $\alpha_K \ln K$, $0.5\beta_{KK}[\ln K]^2$, $\beta_{EK}\ln E \ln K$, $\beta_{DK}\ln D \ln K$ and $\beta_{HK}\ln H \ln K$ are added to (5.3). A quick perusal of (5.3) shows that it is essentially a quadratic approximation to an arbitrary function of the inputs. If we assume constant returns to scale in the case of three inputs, any doubling of all three must double output, so that $\alpha_E + \alpha_D + \alpha_H = 1$ and $\beta_{iE} + \beta_{iD} + \beta_{iH} = 0$ for i = E, D or H. These four restrictions on the specification in (5.3) mean that there are only six independent parameters that describe the technology that transforms the number of workers, their days worked and daily hours into output. Where K is also included, the analogous homogeneity constraints mean that there are ten independent parameters.

Estimates of (5.3) could show that technology restricts employers to use workers, days, and hours in fixed proportions; it could demonstrate that additional workers can easily be substituted for days and hours, but that the latter two must be kept in proportion; or perhaps all three are easily substitutable one for the other. The main thing is that this flexible representation of production allows for any degree of substitution among the three dimensions of labor time and of any of them for capital. It thus imposes no restrictions on the estimates of c_{ij}, the crucial parameters that describe how the relative productivity of the different dimensions of labor responds to changes in their relative quantities (at a given level of cost).

Sources of Data

The ideal way to estimate the parameters in (5.2) and (5.3) is to have information on employment, days, hours, capital stock, and workers' characteristics from a random sample of establishments describing an entire economy. Regrettably no such set of data is available in the United States, Germany or anywhere else. Indeed, sets of data based on surveys of establishments are very few, and most are limited to the increasingly small and unrepresentative manufacturing sector. None of these has the necessary information on both days and daily hours.

The only information available on days and daily hours in the United States is from the Current Population Survey (CPS) May 1991 Supplement, used in chapters 2 and 3, and its predecessors. Thus estimation of the production relationships (5.2) and (5.3) must be based in part on those household data rather than on data from the more appropriate establishment surveys. The strategy for constructing a usable set of data takes the May 1985 and May 1991 CPS supplements and groups all workers by industry (at the three-digit level of disaggregation). For all employees in a particular industry the average days and daily hours on the workers' main jobs are calculated, as are component measures that might represent labor quality, including average years of schooling, ED; average experience (age- schooling- 6), EXP, and the percentage of workers in that industry in the sample who are MALE. (This process excludes workers who classify their main job as one in which they are self-employed.) I then link these household-based measures of D, H and X to published establishment-based data on output and employment (or output, employment, and capital stock) using the industry coding that is common to the two sets of data. Generating a set of data in this way means that the measures of D, H and X imputed to a particular industry are inherently subject to sampling error.

The matching procedure requires combining various sets of three-digit industries from the CPS to match the more highly aggregated establishment-based data. The process yields the three sets of data that I use in the estimation. The first describes manufacturing industries and is based on the May 1985 CPS aggregates matched to data from the 1987 Census of Manufactures.[3] Employment is measured as the total number of employees, which is the most appropriate measure of E to use in estimating a relationship that is based on representations of the days and daily hours of all workers in the industry.[4] Output is measured as value added in the industry, which may obviate any need to worry about how the parameters of interest, the c_{ij}, are affected by interindustry variations in the use of materials. The matching process yields a cross section of 66 manufacturing industries that have at least 25 workers on whom information is available in the May 1985 CPS data on D, H and X for this matched sample. Because no good data on the capital stock are readily available for this sample, the estimates of (5.2) and (5.3) for manufacturing are based only on the three inputs E, D and H.[5]

I also link the CPS data to published National Income and Product Account (NIPA) information on employment (the number of full- and part-time employees) and GNP by industry. Also available from the same basic source are data on the net stock of capital.[6] All private non-farm industries (except private household service) for which complete matches could be found are included in the samples, as for all of them the CPS supplements contained enough workers that measurement problems in D, H and X were likely to be fairly small. The averages from the May 1985 CPS supplement were matched to the NIPA data on E, K and Y for 1985, and those from the May 1991 CPS supplement were matched to NIPA data on E and Y for 1991. (The data on K for that sample are from the last available year, 1989.) The results are samples of 52 industries in 1985 and 53 industries in 1991. The industries are essentially at the two-digit level of aggregation.

One might argue that estimating a production function over units (industries) that are so diverse represents a major departure from the underlying theory of production. I recognize that production functions may differ across the units (just as they may across firms within a small industry) and view the estimates presented here as depicting some average of technologies confronting a variety of combinations of input prices. This rationale is the unstated one for a substantial body of research that estimates production relationships across broad industries. (See, among many examples, Freeman and Medoff 1982; Sosin and Fairchild 1984; and the research on the demand for workers and hours by Ehrenberg and Schumann 1982.)

Statistics describing the three samples of data on industries are contained in tables 5.1U. For each I present the mean, range, and standard deviation of D and H (weighted according to the number of workers in

Table 5.1U1   Descriptive Statistics of Work Time Measures, Manufacturing Industries, 1987

Variable	Mean	Minimum	Maximum	Standard deviation
Employment (000)	262	35	1,144	
Days per week	4.99	4.81	5.16	.069
Hours per day	8.20	7.07	8.96	.268
Number of CPS observations N =11,546		26	825	
Number of industries	66			

NOTE: The data on days and hours are weighted by the number of CPS observations.

Table 5.1U2   Descriptive Statistics of Work Time Measures and Capital Stock, Two-Digit Industries, 1985

Variable	Mean	Minimum	Maximum	Standard deviation
Employment (000)	1,529	46	17,783	
Days per week	4.89	4.60	5.40	.151
Hours per day	7.94	6.84	9.23	.448
Net capital stock per employee (000)	$59.0	$8.0	$580.0	$111.7
Number of CPS observations N = 49,649		39	10,267	
Number of industries	52			

NOTE: The data on days and hours are weighted by the number of CPS observations.

Table 5.1U3   Descriptive Statistics of Work Time Measures and Capital Stock, Two-Digit Industries, 1991

Variable	Mean	Minimum	Maximum	Standard deviation
Employment (000)	1,695	49	19,948	
Days per week	4.89	4.56	5.52	.160
Hours per day	8.02	7.20	9.69	.452
Net capital stock per employee (000)	$58.3	$8.2	$601.3	$112.8
Number of CPS observations N = 50,356		26	9,853	
Number of industries	53			

NOTE: The data on days and hours are weighted by the number of CPS observations.

the CPS supplement on whom the imputed industry average is based). Also included are statistics describing the establishment-based data on industry employment (and on the ratio K/E for the NIPA industries) and the total and interindustry range of the number of observations from the CPS supplement to which the establishment data are linked. Even with the fairly high degree of aggregation implicit in using two-digit industries throughout the private nonfarm sector, tables 5.1U2 and 5.1U3 show that there is some variation in average days per week across industries, and even larger interindustry variation in average daily hours. Though the data on the capital stock per worker show huge variation across industries, their mean seems roughly consistent with general observations.

In the sample of manufacturing industries (containing observations on aggregates of establishments that presumably are less heterogeneous than establishments in the aggregates in the other two samples) the variation in D and H is less than in the two-digit industries. Even here, however, as table 5.1U1 shows, hours range over nearly two per day, but average days worked only vary by ± 0.2 around a mean of almost 5 days per week. The relatively greater variation in the samples containing two-digit industries suggests that there is more hope of obtaining sensible and statistically useful estimates of the production parameters describing them than there may be for the sample of manufacturing industries.

Before turning to the estimates of (5.2) and (5.3), it is worth considering whether industries that employ long workdays also employ workers many days per week, or whether instead D and H are independent across industries. This comparison asks at the level of aggregates of establishments the same question that we analyzed at the level of individual workers in tables 2.4. Remember from those tables that days and daily hours are significantly positively correlated across individuals, though the correlations are quite low. For the 66 manufacturing industries the weighted correlation of D and H across industries is only 0.20, significantly nonzero only at the 90 percent level of confidence. Figure 5.1U1 presents a scatter of the pairs of days and daily hours for each industry, with the sizes of the circles commensurate with the weights (number of CPS observations) underlying each. Even excluding the outlier at $H = 7.067$ (newspaper printing and publishing), only a slight positive relationship is apparent ($r = 0.17$); and deleting the outlier at $D = 4.8077$ (canning fruits and vegetables) also does not greatly improve the fit ($r = 0.23$). There is little tendency for those small manufacturing industries where workers put in long days to be the same ones where workers labor unusually many days per week.[7]

Figure 5.1U1   Daily Hours and Days per Week, Manufacturing Industries, 1987

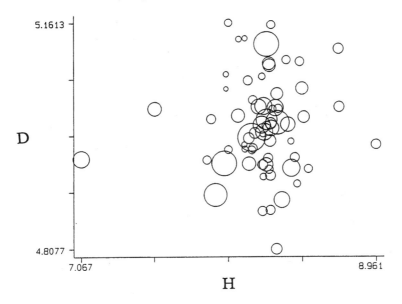

The story is much different for the two-digit nonfarm industries. As figures 5.1U2 and 5.1U3 show, there seems to be a strong positive relationship between average daily hours and days worked per week in an industry. Including all the industries in the data for 1985, the weighted correlation coefficient is 0.63; in the 1991 data it is 0.51, both significantly positive at the 99 percent level. Removing the outliers with unusually low days (health services in 1985, membership organizations in 1991) makes the impression of a close positive relation between D and H even stronger: The correlations rise to 0.83 and 0.82 in the 1985 and 1991 data respectively. Across the whole economy those subaggregates where workers labor long each day are those where they also work more days per week.

Figure 5.1U2   Daily Hours and Days per Week, Private Nonfarm Industries, 1985

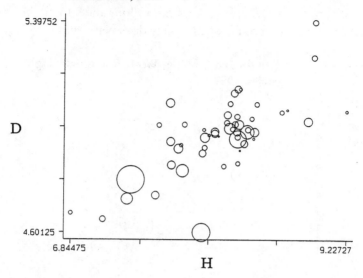

Figure 5.1U3   Daily Hours and Days per Week, Private Nonfarm Industries, 1991

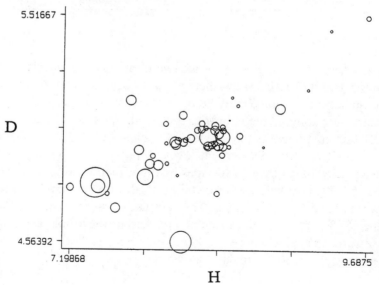

The theme of this monograph has been the comparison of unusual dimensions of work time in the United States and Germany. Ideally the same estimates and tables used here to analyze the determinants of the demand for workers, days, and daily hours in the United States could be constructed for German industries as well. Regrettably, the nature of the GSOEP prevents that: there are only 27 "branches of economic activity" in what in the United States would be classified in the private nonfarm sector that have more than 25 respondents in the 1990 wave of the GSOEP. A finer industrial classification would not really solve the problem, since with a sample only one-tenth the size of a U.S. May CPS supplement still greater disaggregation would result in most industries having very few workers on whom to base estimates of average days and daily hours by industry.

We can compare some descriptive statistics on the distribution of average days and daily hours in Germany and examine how these are correlated across industries. Table 5.1G shows statistics that are analogous to those presented in tables 5.1U2 and 5.1U3. The similarities between the German and U.S. data are striking. Implicit for both countries is that differences in average days across industries are much smaller than differences in average hours. That is true whether one compares standard deviations or examines the ranges. As was apparent from the analysis of the data on individuals for Germany, so too in data aggregated by industry there appear to be more opportunities for flexibility in scheduling daily hours than in scheduling days of work.

Table 5.1G   Descriptive Statistics of Work Time Measures, Two-Digit Industries, 1990

Variable	Mean	Minimum	Maximum	Standard deviation
Days per week	5.05	4.86	5.52	.111
Hours per day	7.84	5.51	8.96	.494
Number of GSOEP observations N = 3,690		30	438	
Number of industries	27			

NOTE: The data on days and hours are weighted by the number of GSOEP observations.

As in the data describing private nonfarm industries in the United States, in the German data average days and daily hours of work are positively correlated across industries ($r = 0.35$, significant at the 95 percent level). The distribution of industry averages is shown in figure 5.1G, again using the numbers of observations from the underlying household data as weights. The positive correlation is apparent; moreover, it would be substantially higher ($r = 0.51$) if the extreme outlier with average daily hours of only 5.51 (trash removal) were itself removed from the sample.

Figure 5.1G   Daily Hours and Days per Week, Private Nonfarm Industries, Germany, 1990

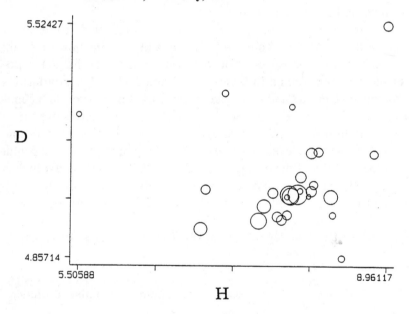

With only 27 usable two-digit private nonfarm industries in 1990 it does not make sense to match the GSOEP data to published information on industrial employment and output to estimate (5.2) and (5.3). That conclusion is underscored when we notice that not all the 27 match the classification under which measures of output are published for Germany. Nonetheless, the similarity of the distributions and correlations of days and daily hours across industries should give a bit of hope that results for the United States might be applicable in Germany (and perhaps elsewhere too).

Estimates of Production Relations Among Employees, Days, and Hours

In this section I present the results of estimating (5.2) and (5.3), both with and without the capital stock in the case of the NIPA industries. These are representations of production based on the sets of data I have constructed describing employment, days of work, daily hours, and the capital stock in U.S. industries. In addition to showing the estimates of the α_i and β_{ij} from (5.3) I also discuss the calculated values of the c_{ij} (the responses of relative input prices to imposed changes in the relative amounts of the inputs) that are based on them. These partial elasticities of complementarity allow us to draw inferences about substitution possibilities among these dimensions of labor time.

The first column in table 5.2U1 and the first two columns in tables 5.2U2-3 present estimates of equation (5.2) for the data describing manufacturing industries in 1987 and private nonfarm industries in 1985 and 1991. The second column in table 5.2U1 and the final two columns in tables 5.2U2-3 show the estimates of equation (5.3). All the estimates are weighted by the number of observations from the CPS that underlay the calculations of days and daily hours for each industry. The first thing to note is that the translog specification clearly dominates the extended Cobb-Douglas model: In each set of data, and whether or not a measure of the stock of capital is included, the $\bar{R}^2$ is higher for the corresponding translog specification. Clearly, the implicit assumptions of a constant and identical degree of substitution (equal partial elasticities of complementarity within all pairs of inputs) are rejected by the data. The substantially higher $\bar{R}^2$ in the NIPA data when a measure of the capital stock is included demonstrate the value of obtaining such data.

In the more appropriate translog specification the constraint that days and daily hours are treated identically, i.e., that employers view weekly hours as *DH* for purposes of planning production, is strongly rejected by the data in all three samples. This answers one of the central questions posed in the introduction: It is clear that, if we use an appropriately general description of technology, it is incorrect to write the utilization of workers as *DH*. Workdays and daily hours are treated differently in production. The estimates also imply that these two are not equally easily substitutable for workers. Thus the huge array of previous research, that due to the unavailability of data concentrates on substitution between workers and weekly hours, misses the crucial technological fact that employers do not behave as if days and daily hours affect output in this specific manner. By expanding our notions of the dimensions of work time in production we learn something about employers' demand for labor.

Table 5.2U1   Estimates of Production Models, Manufacturing Industries, 1987 (Dependent Variable is ln(Output))

Coefficient	Generalized Cobb-Douglas	Translog
α_E	.845	2.786
	(.05)	(0.99)
α_D	1.118	−7.803
	(3.14)	(4.20)
α_H	2.116	6.043
	(1.24)	(3.49)
β_{EE}		0.082
		(0.095)
β_{DD}		−5.691
		(3.92)
β_{HH}		10.600
		(4.11)
β_{ED}		4.043
		(1.78)
β_{EH}		−4.085
		(1.78)
β_{DH}		−1.192
		(0.92)
$\overline{R}^2$	.869	.878

NOTE: Standard errors in parentheses. Also included in each equation are variables measuring the average education of workers in the industry, their labor-market experience (age − education − 6) and its square, and the fraction of male workers in the industry.

Table 5.2U2   Estimates of Production Models, Two-Digit Industries, 1985 (Dependent Variable is ln(Output))

Coefficient	Generalized Cobb-Douglas		Translog	
	Without K	With K	Without K	With K
α_E	0.979	0.71	−0.982	−1.500
	(0.07)	(0.06)	(1.22)	(0.70)
α_D	6.629	−1.679	17.324	−8.764
	(3.59)	(2.86)	(7.85)	(6.93)
α_H	−0.128	1.653	−15.316	10.823
	(1.84)	(1.34)	(6.87)	(6.44)
α_K		0.385		0.441
		(.06)		(0.82)
β_{EE}			0.189	0.250
			(0.117)	(0.08)
β_{DD}			10.297	1.936
			(4.15)	(2.38)
β_{HH}			1.494	0.870
			(2.60)	(1.64)
β_{KK}				0.233
				(0.06)
β_{ED}			−2.256	−3.922
			(1.41)	(0.80)
β_{EH}			2.164	3.934
			(1.39)	(0.78)
β_{DH}			−2.887	−0.717
			(1.01)	(0.52)
β_{EK}				−0.137
				(0.06)
β_{DK}				3.672
				(0.98)
β_{HK}				−3.652
				(0.98)
$\overline{R}^2$	.848	.922	.853	.968

NOTE: Standard errors in parentheses.

Table 5.2U3 Estimates of Production Models, Two-Digit Industries, 1991 (Dependent Variable is ln(Output))

Coefficient	Generalized Cobb-Douglas		Translog	
	Without K	With K	Without K	With K
α_E	0.967	0.659	−1.132	−0.630
	(0.07)	(0.07)	(1.23)	(0.59)
α_D	6.219	−0.413	23.013	−6.497
	(3.21)	(2.52)	(8.06)	(6.33)
α_H	2.953	2.364	−20.856	8.321
	(1.77)	(1.28)	(7.04)	(5.80)
α_K		0.406		−0.194
		(0.06)		(0.62)
β_{EE}			0.099	0.167
			(0.107)	(0.06)
β_{DD}			14.944	2.054
			(4.14)	(2.40)
β_{HH}			0.771	0.169
			(2.66)	(1.48)
β_{KK}				0.283
				(0.05)
β_{ED}			−3.577	−3.452
			(1.40)	(0.62)
β_{EH}			3.527	3.529
			(1.38)	(0.605)
β_{DH}			−3.889	−0.604
			(1.04)	(0.50)
β_{EK}				−0.160
				(0.05)
β_{DK}				3.029
				(0.69)
β_{HK}				−3.010
				(0.69)
$\overline{R}^2$	.842	.919	.857	.976

NOTE: Standard errors in parentheses.

In the results based on the extended Cobb-Douglas form the old finding that the combined marginal effects of additional days and daily hours exceed that of additional workers appears to be present in the manufacturing data and in one of the NIPA data sets whether or not capital is included, and in the other only if capital is excluded. Why returns to the time of workers should exceed that to their number is not clear. Were the data describing changes in a time series, one might argue that the results reflect disequilibria that indicate firms are responding to shocks that lead to observed differences in productivities of inputs whose costs presumably differ little at the margin. With our cross-section data, however, this interpretation does not seem likely. A more satisfying explanation is that there are indivisibilities in hours and days that generate discrete drops in their marginal productivities as additional units are added. Thus adding an extra day of work or another daily hour per worker may be unprofitable for the typical firm, even though the last day or hour in use is more productive than would be an equally costly amount of labor services added through hiring.

The estimates of the parameters describing the translog production approximations (5.3) do not tell us very much by themselves. In such models the high correlations among the variables (remember, linear and quadratic terms in each input are included along with all cross-product terms) usually guarantee that some of the parameters are not significant. As is also common in the literature on production functions, the homogeneity constraints imposed on the α_i and the β_{ij} are not satisfied.[8]

Although the tables do not list the estimates, the equations described by columns (1) and (2) also include the measures of labor quality, X. These are specified as:

$$(5.4)\quad g(X) = \gamma_1 ED + \gamma_2 EXP - \gamma_3 EXP^2 + \gamma_4 MALE.$$

The estimated γ_i are positive in all three samples, as expected. Moreover, in all three the quadratic in experience generally peaks around 25 years (age 43), roughly comparable to what the evidence from equations describing earnings suggests is the peak of the age-earnings relationship (and by inference the age-productivity relationship). Having a workforce with one extra year of schooling increases output in an industry by between 25 and 35 percent in the data. Since standard estimates of the rate of return to education are far below this (although some recent estimates, e.g., Ashenfelter and Krueger 1994, and Butcher and Case 1994 produce numbers that are almost this implausibly large), by inference extra education does more to raise productivity than is captured in the returns reaped by individual workers. Finally, and also somewhat difficult to credit, moving from an all-female to an all-male workforce would implicitly raise output by 10 percent in manufacturing, which does not seem unreasonable; but the effects in the data on private nonfarm industries, above 30 percent, are hard to credit. Since the estimates are unchanged when K is added to the model, this possible measure of labor quality cannot be capturing some of the effects of omitted data on interindustry differences in the stock of capital with which they may be positively correlated. A more likely explanation is that they could be reflecting a greater gender difference in labor costs that is passed forward into output prices in these industries.

The partial elasticities of complementarity among the three dimensions of labor input (or among these and capital) are shown in table 5.3U. Each elasticity is based on the parameters describing the productivity of the particular inputs under consideration, e.g., the calculation of c_{DH} does not depend on the estimates of any of the parameters in (5.3) that involve E (or K).[9] Consider first the estimates of the models that exclude the capital stock. All the elasticities are fairly substantial, implying that a decrease in supply along one of the dimensions of labor time would generate a good-sized change in its productivity relative to that of the other two dimensions. Except for the surprising negative estimate of c_{EH} in manufacturing, the estimates all imply that this change would be negative. Obversely, an increase in input along any dimension of labor use would raise the relative returns along the other dimensions. The estimates of the elasticities when the model is expanded to include a measure of the stock of capital do not change that greatly, *except* for the measure of substitution between E and D in the data for 1985.

Most interesting in the results is the constancy of the estimates of c_{DH} across the samples: Each implies that a 10 percent increase in hours per day relative to days per week lowers the relative productivity of hours by roughly 10 percent.[10] At a fixed cost of output the relative productivities of different dimensions of labor input, and their implicit prices, are fairly responsive to changes in their relative supplies. When we add a measure of the stock of capital to the model based on data covering private industries, the estimates of c_{DH} remain very similar to what they are in the simpler models. The results indicate that employers do not use days and hours in fixed proportions. Taken together with the evidence that the data reject treating days and hours as the simple multiple *DH*, this finding shows the gains to be attained from treating these new dimensions of time on the job as separate inputs with different costs and different degrees of substitution for other inputs.

Table 5.3U   Partial Elasticities of Complementarity (c_{ij})

	Model excludes K		Model includes K		
Sample	Days	Hours	Days	Hours	Capital
Manufacturing, 1987					
		–			
Employment	1.616	1.756			
Days		0.824			
Private industry, 1985					
			–		
Employment	0.816	1.736	0.878	2.599	0.000028
Days		0.818		0.866	0.00045
Hours					–0.00027
Private industry, 1991					
Employment	0.648	1.456	1.791	2.582	0.000018
Days		0.903		1.038	–0.000041
Hours					–0.00013

Simulating the Impact of Some Labor Market Regulations

Both of the policies that I discuss in this section impose restrictions on employers' use of labor inputs and have as their chief goal increasing the demand for employees. The difficulty always is that, even though such policies may attain their primary goal, they may do so at a high cost in terms of the total demand for labor in all its dimensions, and thus in the total amount of output and eventually living standards. The policies that I analyze here are characterizations of what might be imposed. For example, while many people have proposed requiring that overtime penalties become applicable after 7-1/2 hours per day, no one has seriously proposed outlawing the use of daily hours in excess of that amount. Similarly, while limiting the workweek to four days has been considered, no bans on workweeks of five or more days have been suggested. The simulations here thus characterize extreme forms of policies that have been discussed seriously. As such, they provide upper limits on the extent to which the policies would increase employment (and the amount of output that might have to be foregone to achieve those gains).

Policies that limit daily hours or days per week are essentially non-linear: The extent of the constraint on firms' choices cannot be inferred from observations on average hours or days in the entire economy. For example, even if the average firm in each industry has a workweek of 7-1/2 hours, it is quite likely that firms within many or even all industries have longer workweeks. In this case we would infer no impact of the policy if we used industry data, even though it clearly would have some effect. The direction of the bias resulting from basing estimates of the employment effects of such policies on aggregated data is unclear, as it depends on the underlying distributions of daily hours and days among firms within each industry. Here again, if we had establishment- or firm-level data, this problem would be obviated.

A final difficulty is that we must assume that the policy is fully enforced, so that any simulated change in behavior would be observed if the policy were imposed. There is substantial evidence that regulatory labor laws are not enforced completely, and some evidence (Ehrenberg and Schumann 1982) that American employers do not fully comply with the overtime provisions of the Fair Labor Standards Act. For this reason the estimated effects of imposing the restrictions on days or daily hours will be upper bounds.

The first archetypal policy that I analyze is a requirement that all workweeks consist of four or fewer days (similar to the proposal in Poor 1973; to suggestions for stimulating employment in France in the early 1990s, and to a proposal early in 1995 by the German trade union movement).[11] The effects of this and any other limitation on days can be seen by taking the estimates of (5.3), imposing a change in D and calculating the implied changes in E and H that would be required to maintain output at its current level. Here the imposed percentage change in D is equal to the average amount by which days exceed four. In the three samples this excess averages 20, 18, and 18 percent respectively. In manufacturing, this proposal would have its biggest effect on iron and steel foundries, tires and inner tubes, and miscellaneous transportation equipment. Among two-digit private industries the largest burden would be borne by coal mining, oil, and gas extraction, water transport and textile manufacturing.

The second simulation asks about the changes in employment and/or days of work that could be produced by a mandated cut in daily workhours to 7-1/2. This is similar to the reductions that were imposed in Germany (to 37 hours per week) in the 1980s (though, of course, here I assume that no hours can be worked beyond the mandated limit). Given the existing distributions of daily workhours across industries, such a mandate would have produced cuts of 9, 6 and 7 percent in average daily hours in the three samples used in this chapter. In manufacturing this would have an especially heavy impact on cement products, dairy products, and beverage manufacturing. Among two-digit private industries the biggest effect would be on the same industries that are most affected by a mandated cut in days per week (a reflection of the high correlation that we showed existed between days and daily hours across these broad industries).

For each sample I present in the left-hand side of table 5.4U the trade-off that the economy would face if the workweek were restricted to no more than four days. This trade-off, written generally as $\Delta\ln E = a - b\Delta\ln H$, shows the choices between higher employment and/or longer workdays needed to maintain output after the cut in days worked. In the case of private industry in 1985 I also present estimates of this trade-off based on the expanded model that included measures of the stock of capital. I assume that the trade-off is effected only through the dimensions of labor, so that the capital stock cannot vary. Since other evidence indicates that additional capital raises the productivity of labor, for this reason too the calculations overstate the potential for increasing employment. For 1991 the expanded model yielded estimates that were not usable for the simulations, since the implied effect of additional days on output was negative.

Except for the private nonfarm sample in 1991, the evidence suggests that the decline in output attendant upon cutting the number of workdays per week could be made up by equal percentage increases in employment or in daily hours. If we include capital in the model for private industry, the results suggest that the lost output would be recovered with smaller increases in employment than in daily hours. That is an encouraging finding; but the real problem that the results point up is that the simulations that do not include the stock of capital suggest that the likely loss in output would be huge, on the order of 65 percent.

Table 5.4U   Policy Trade-Offs for Selected Limits on Work Time

Data	Limit to 4 days per week	Limit to 7.5 hours per day
Manufacturing, 1987	$\Delta \ln E = 1.01 - 1.03\Delta \ln H$	$\Delta \ln E = 0.09 - 4.57\Delta \ln D$
Private industry, 1985		
Capital excluded:	$\Delta \ln E = 1.09 - 1.30\Delta \ln H$	$\Delta \ln E = 0.08 - 5.41\Delta \ln D$
Capital included:	$\Delta \ln E = 0.04 - 0.24\Delta \ln H$	$\Delta \ln E = 0.15 - 0.20\Delta \ln D$
Private industry, 1991	$\Delta \ln E = 1.05 - 3.95\Delta \ln H$	$\Delta \ln E = 0.28 - 5.19\Delta \ln D$

A mandated cut in workdays of "only" 20 percent makes a 65 percent cut in output far too large to be believable. That this, the only available simulation of the impact of cutting workdays, suggests such a large drop in output should, however, give some pause to those who advocate mandating or even giving incentives for longer weekends. Even when the capital stock is included we see that the loss in output is still 4 percent, small but not tiny. Implicit in the simulation is the assumption that job slots could be created, or the workday lengthened sufficiently to keep output constant after the mandated cut in workdays. That is almost certainly incorrect. Instead, some of the impact of the cut would be in the form of lower output and reduced living standards, as the imposed departure from employers' most efficient use of the various dimensions of work time induces additional inefficiency in production. Jobs might well be created; but the cost in output of limiting days worked appears to be high.

The right-hand side of table 5.4U presents the results of simulating the impact of the mandatory reduction in daily hours. In each case this restriction generates a trade-off that could be met by increasing employment or adding days of work while holding output constant, according to the relationship $\Delta\ln E = a - b\Delta\ln D$. The trade-off is not one-for-one: The models without the measure of the capital stock imply that days of work need only be raised slightly, between 1.5 and 5 percent (presumably, given the indivisibility of the workday, raised only in a few firms or for a small percent of the workforce) to maintain output if hours are cut. When capital is included the reverse conclusion is obtained, that it would be relatively easy to make up the lost output by increasing employment but difficult to do so by raising daily hours. As in the first simulation there is no reason to expect that this response would be complete. Some of any possible increase in employment would be dissipated in the form of reduced output economywide with a consequent drop in per-capita living standards.

There is some conflict among the simulation results, particularly when we compare the results from the models for private industry in 1985 without and with the capital stock included. Nonetheless, the simulations do tell one consistent story: Mandating reductions in workdays per week (or in daily hours) requires large changes in employment and/or daily hours (days per week) if output losses are to be avoided. Given the costs that such mandates impose on the economy, these estimates of aggregate production functions imply that it is not likely that the entire drop in output will be made up.

What Have We Learned?

This chapter has provided the first inquiry into how employers treat various dimensions of work time in production. It provides fairly strong evidence that:

In industries where workdays are long the workweek generally consists of unusually many workdays.

Employers do not treat all hours in the workweek, consisting of days worked and daily hours, as equally productive. Days and daily hours cannot be aggregated.

The detrimental side-effects from cutting the workweek to

stimulate employment demand may be smaller if cuts in daily hours are mandated than if employers are required to reduce the number of workdays.

The general point of all these results is that only by treating days and daily hours separately can we hope to infer how imposed changes in the price or quantity of either of them will affect employment.

The analysis for the United States must be viewed as an initial step in studying employers' demands for these three dimensions of labor input. The inferences are only tentative, but they are suggestive. Though there is a fairly high positive correlation of days and daily hours across industries, some substitution between them does occur. This suggests that a higher overtime premium applied on hours per day (as in Germany) will have different effects from one applied on hours per week (as in the United States). If policy makers wish to stimulate the demand for workers (create jobs) by restricting work time, limiting daily hours seems more advisable than limiting the number of workdays per week. One must remember, however, that even this less costly restriction, though it may raise employment, will surely reduce total production and thus real living standards.

NOTES

1. These were proposed regularly during recessions in the United States through the 1980s, with many specifying double pay for overtime hours and/or reductions in the normal *weekly* hours at which the penalty applies, usually to 35 hours.

2. Much of this literature is also summarized in Hamermesh (1993, chapter 3). An unusual study in this area, and one of the few to use microeconomic data, is Gerlach and Hübler (1988).

3. Based on Bureau of the Census, *Census of Manufactures*, 1987, volume 1-4, table 3.

4. One could disasggregate further by treating full-time and part-time employees separately and including the total number of each, their days and daily hours, as separate inputs. In theory this would generate additional knowledge about substitution among days, workers, and daily hours. In practice estimates based on equations like (5.3) provide very little useful information if more than 4 or 5 inputs are included, mainly because the need to include the quadratic terms and the products of each pair of inputs generates severe problems of multicollinearity.

5. This approach to constructing a set of matched household-establishment data for use in estimating a production function is similar in spirit to that in Grant and Hamermesh (1981).

6. The data on employment and output are published in *Survey of Current Business*, volume 66, July 1986, tables 6.1 and 6.6b, and volume 73, August 1993, tables 6.1 and 6.4C. The data on net capital stock are from Bureau of Economic Affairs, *Fixed Reproducible Tangible Wealth in the United States, 1925-89,* Washington, 1993.

7. Nor is this low correlation the result of interindustry differences in the extent of unionization. Partial correlations of D and H were estimated for this sample adjusted for the percentage of

workers in the industry who were covered by collective bargaining in 1987 (from Curme et al. 1990). The partial correlation coefficient between D and H was 0.14.

8. Despite this failure the estimates in the tables all generate positive-definite matrices of second partial derivatives of output with respect to the inputs evaluated at the sample means.

9. The calculation involves only the first, second, and cross-partial derivatives of Y with respect to the two inputs i and j included in the particular c_{ij} (Hamermesh 1993, equation 2.35).

10. In a two-factor model this would imply that a Cobb-Douglas specification is appropriate. That $c_{DH} \approx 1$ in this multifactor model does not imply that the elasticity of substitution equals 1; and the empirical superiority of the translog specification demonstrates that such a simple specification is an inappropriate description of technology.

11. See *New York Times,* November 22, 1993, p. 1.

CHAPTER 6

Summing Up

We have examined a wide variety of issues involving how days of work, hours of work, and daily schedules are determined in the United States and Germany. Though these issues are general and of obvious importance in understanding behavior in the labor market, they have received surprisingly little attention from economists and other social scientists, partly because of a shortage of necessary data. This monograph thus provides the first comprehensive evidence on these outcomes in the United States or elsewhere. More important, because it is explicitly comparative and examines exactly the same issue in exactly the same way wherever the data from the two countries allow it, we can be fairly sure that any regularities observed in both countries result from more than merely the institutional idiosyncrasies of a particular economy. This means that, unlike most studies of labor markets, we will have produced more than an econometric case study. Examining the issues for both countries also offers the obvious advantage of providing opportunities to compare how the outcomes differ internationally and to attempt to link the differences to differences in institutional structures.

Some Apparent Facts Describing Days, Hours, and Work Schedules

Probably the most obvious, yet in some ways surprising fact to emerge from the analyses is the ubiquity of unusual daily schedules and combinations of days and hours. Large percentages of the labor forces in both countries work in the evenings (between 7 and 10PM) or at night (between 10PM and 6AM): On the typical workday roughly one-sixth of all workers put in some time regularly in the evening on their main or (among the few moonlighters) secondary job, and nearly one-tenth do so at night. The stereotypic image of the 9 to 5 worker describes the majority of labor force participants in both countries, but unusual work times are more prevalent than one might expect.

Our image of the 9 to 5 schedule is combined with our view of the 5-day workweek. Five-day weeks are by far the most common; but over one-fourth of all American workers, and one-seventh of Germans, work fewer or more days. The notion of the 8-hour day is also prevalent, even though only two-thirds of workers in each country put in between 7 and 8 on their typical workday. What is also interesting is that small, but not tiny proportions of workers in the two countries are working fewer than 7 hours on more than 5 days, or more than 8 hours on fewer than 5 days.

We speak of people who work in the evenings or at nights as being on the evening or night shift. Yet the majority of people who are at work between 7 and 10PM do not view themselves as being on the evening shift when asked about it and are not classified as evening-shift workers when their total work schedules are examined; and many of them are working during the daytime on the same job. Similarly, the majority of people at work between 10PM and 6AM are not night-shift workers. Taken together, these findings suggest that the notion of "shift" is far too rigid to be of use, and that at the very least for purposes of analyzing workers' behavior we need to focus on the more complex question of the actual times of day that people are at work.

By separating weekly schedules into days and daily hours we have been able to examine how these vary over the life cycle. The well-known inverse U-shaped relation of weekly (and annual) hours to age has been one of the fundamental facts that shows the consistency of life-cycle behavior with economic incentives (the inverse U-shaped age-earnings relation). The evidence here suggests that the life cycle in weekly hours results mostly from the life cycle in daily hours: Days worked per week vary relatively less with age than do daily hours.

We have also discovered a number of facts about the burden of work at unusual times of the day or of unusual combinations of days and hours. This burden is unsurprisingly borne disproportionately by groups with relatively little human capital—by the less-educated and the young (by inference the less-skilled). In the United States minority workers, especially blacks, are more likely to work unusually many days given their weekly workhours, and they are especially likely to be working evenings or nights. In Germany the results are less clear, but there is some weak evidence that immigrants are similarly burdened. If we take the view that we care about American minorities or the less-skilled *as groups* rather than individuals, these findings should concern us, since they show that as groups they work on relatively undesirable schedules. Within these groups, however, there is substantial turnover in the identities of the particular workers who work unusual combinations of days or hours or who work at unusual times of the day. *Across individuals* the burden of work at times that most people view as inferior is less long-lasting than is implied by comparisons among groups of workers.

An immense body of economic research on labor supply and a substantial literature on labor demand too has been based on the distinction between workers and hours (usually weekly) of work. Both literatures have lumped together days and daily hours into the aggregate weekly hours, implicitly assuming that the behavior of days and daily hours in response to other factors is identical. A uniform lesson from all of the analyses in this volume is that this aggregation is incorrect. The demographic correlates of days and daily hours differ in some cases in the directions of their effects; and in many cases the sizes of effects in the same direction differ substantially. Employers too do not treat days and hours the same way when deciding how to respond to shocks to their costs.

A major concern of labor economists and of sociologists of work is the effect of family structure and characteristics on labor market outcomes. The most interesting new finding in this area from the research in this study is the apparent complementarity of the timing of work of wives and husbands. Couples with both spouses working prefer to enjoy their leisure together at the same time. This nexus nearly disappears when the exigencies of child care imposed by the presence of young children are added to the couple's decision making.

It is well known that the presence of young children reduces mothers' hours of work outside the home. The evidence suggests that the negative effects in the United States, though not in Germany, are much bigger on days of work than on daily hours. This suggests the importance of arranging child care: it may be easier to add an extra hour of care each day than to arrange another day of care. Among men, both days and daily hours are increased when there are young children in the household.

A consistent result is the greater relative variability of hours than of days across labor force participants. Multivariate analyses also show that days vary relatively less than do hours in response to differences among individuals in nearly all of their demographic and economic characteristics. Finally, there is more interindustry variation in average hours than there is in average days in both the United States and Germany. This remarkable agreement along so many dimensions and in both countries would seem to suggest the conclusion that firms find it more difficult to alter days than hours, and that workers have stronger preferences for the same days of work as other workers than they do for hours similar to those of their fellows. This conclusion would ignore, however, the results from chapter 4 that workers find it no more necessary to change jobs to alter their workdays than they do to alter daily workhours.

How can we reconcile this apparently partially contradictory set of findings? Together they can be rationalized by the following underlying behavior: Workers' tastes for days of work are more tightly bunched than their tastes for daily hours, perhaps because of their greater desire to concentrate their leisure time on standard days off when other family members and other people are enjoying leisure. (This accords with the finding on the complementarity of the timing of husbands' and wives' leisure.) Because of this firms find it much more difficult to alter standard daily schedules than they do standard scheduled daily hours. Nonetheless, they find it equally easy to alter the schedules of those few workers who do wish to change their days of work as those of the other few workers who wish to change their daily hours.

The correlation of days worked and daily hours among individual workers is quite low, even for workers within the same broad industry: knowing, for example, that a person works many days tells us little about whether he or she works long days. Across industries, however, the correlation of days and daily hours is quite high. This apparent contradiction is easily reconciled. Individuals' preferences for schedules are quite heterogeneous. Technologies regarding work time may also differ across and within industries, but certain industries require both long days and long weeks. Workers' tastes are matched to technologies in such a way that the outcomes reflect both worker heterogeneity in their desired days and hours and employers' requirements for schedules that involve long (short) days and long (short) daily hours simultaneously.

Similarities and Differences in the Timing of Work

In the previous section most of the conclusions were based on results that were general in both the United States and Germany. Throughout the monograph I have shown other similarities between patterns of work timing in the two countries that are worth noting, that have implications for inferring how labor markets in developed economies function, and that can increase our understanding of labor market behavior in the two countries. In both nations roughly seven-eighths of the workforce maintain regular days and daily hours of work. In them the distributions of workers by daily hours of work are remarkably similar once one ignores workers on very long hours in the United States. In both, roughly 20 percent of workers perform some of their work on Saturdays; and the fractions of men at work in the evening, or at night, are the same in both countries.

These similarities could arise because the underlying distributions of workers' tastes are similar in the two countries. They could arise because technologies are easily transferred across borders and consumers' demands in the two countries are sufficiently similar to make the distributions of goods and services that are produced similar. It may be that the similarities result from a combination of these underlying characteristics. The appropriate way to examine these possibilities is to use a set of matched establishment-household data that contains information on work schedules. Unfortunately no such data exist, so that discriminating among these causes must await additional work based on as yet nonexistent data.

There are also some interesting differences in the timing of work between the two countries, disparities that suggest some underlying differences in behavior between the United States and Germany. Days of work are much more standard in Germany than in the United States, with the 5-day week being much more the norm. Whether or not people change jobs from one year to the next, individual variation in daily hours of work and in days worked per week across years is much less in Germany than in the United States. These differences imply a greater flexibility in the scheduling of work in the United States. This characteristic may allow the U.S. economy to react to shocks, such as sharp increases in energy prices, so as to absorb detrimental effects on the labor market more readily than does the German labor market (or perhaps Western European economies more generally). An external shock that reduces the demand for goods that are produced using a particular concatenation of days and daily hours is likely to be met with fewer inflationary pressures in the United States, for American workers can apparently be induced more easily to alter their schedules to meet the shift in the relative demand for days and hours.

There are also some interesting differences between the two labor forces in women's patterns of work. More women in Germany work more than 5 days per week than in the United States; but more also work fewer than 7 hours per day. German women's choices about daily hours and days per week are much more sensitive to the presence of young children than are those of their American counterparts; but in the two countries a woman's likelihood of working evenings or nights is roughly equally responsive to the presence of young children at home.

Some of these differences are explicable by the underlying substantially greater labor force attachment of American women. We know from much research within the United States (and elsewhere) that the participation of women who have been more closely attached to the labor force is less responsive to changes in their family circumstances. That being the case, it is not surprising that we find German women's work schedules changing more when they have children. That German women are more likely to work short hours on many days than American women may result from differences in the structure of school and preschool opportunities for their children.

Policy Issues and Problems

The most immediate issue of policy for which the results here are relevant is the problem of job creation. The issue is likely to be especially pressing in those economies and at those times when unemployment has been persistently high, as in Western Europe in the mid-1990s. Assume, as seems reasonable in Europe though perhaps less so in the United States, that a political determination has been made to intervene in the labor market in an attempt to expand employment. Let us also take it as given that no other policy to create jobs and reduce unemployment is politically feasible and likely to be effective, so that cutting daily hours and/or days comes under serious consideration. The findings in this monograph suggest most importantly that cutting weekly workhours in general will not have the same job-creation effects and economic costs as cutting daily hours. That in turn will not generate the same benefits or costs as a policy of reducing work time by reducing days of work. Our evidence suggests that, if one must cut standard work time in the hope of increasing employment demand by reducing the relative cost of workers compared to days and hours, cutting daily hours would generate fewer costs (in terms of efficiency) than would cutting the number of workdays.

This discussion ignores the very real possibility that such mandated costs could so increase the cost of labor that scale effects actually reduce the total demand for workers despite the substitution of workers for days and hours. It also says nothing about any possible welfare losses that might be incurred as incentives are offered that shift society away from the expression of workers' preferences about days and daily hours. On the other hand, it does not deal with welfare gains that might be produced by mandating cuts in days of work in economies (perhaps the United States) where one might argue (see Schor 1991) that the economy is in a low-level equilibrium involving unusually high annual workhours. All it says is: If you must give employers incentives to cut hours of work, you may be able to create jobs at lower cost by providing incentives or mandating cuts in daily hours rather than by cutting days of work.

The evidence in chapters 2 and 3 makes it abundantly clear that having children does not just alter the amount of effort that people supply to the labor market, as has been shown by vast numbers of previous studies. It also alters the timing of work among people whose total hours in the market are otherwise identical. In particular, the presence of young children induces parents to substitute toward working times that are usually associated with people who possess small endowments of human capital. Most of the effect in the United States is on days of work, while in Germany the effects on days and daily hours are roughly equal when very young children are present. That couples' choices of market hours are shifted away from what they would choose in the absence of young children suggests another dimension along which births affect parents' behavior. In all cases the burdens are borne especially by mothers.

Are these effects a social problem about which one should be concerned? On the one hand, one could easily view them as a cost that people have chosen to bear in order to obtain the satisfaction of having children. Simply because people seem to be worse off in one dimension does not imply that a choice has made them worse off overall or that there is a justification for government intervention. Having demonstrated that changes in work schedules are an additional cost of children, however, I have also demonstrated that they represent an additional disincentive to fertility. Moreover, most governments do expend resources on child care, so that we have a *fait accompli* on which we need to offer evidence to help the policy meet its goals at the lowest cost to economic welfare. That being the case, the results of this monograph suggest very strongly that day-care subsidies in the United States should be focused on reducing mothers' costs of working additional days and less so on the costs of additional daily hours. For mothers, the fixed costs of work are daily fixed costs. Subsidies to ease the burden of child care should recognize this by tilting toward offering aid more on a per workday than on a per workhour basis.

The Timing of Work—A Fruitful Area of Inquiry

The timing of work must be determined in every society, either through the evolution of its institutions or by government fiat. Given its pervasiveness and its importance for a variety of labor market policies, it is remarkable how little attention economists have paid to this issue. This monograph has not made any discoveries about the fundamental determinants of the timing of work. It has, however, discovered a wide range of hitherto unknown facts, some of which may describe labor markets in developed economies generally rather than in the United

States or Germany alone. Learning these new facts is the first step on the road to understanding the origins of patterns of the timing of work.

A fundamental rule of economic decision making is that one should invest one's energies where they yield the highest marginal product. Research in the area of labor supply, work effort, and the use of time has become increasingly abstruse and focused on econometric fine points. At the same time we know very little about the timing of work and work schedules. This simple decision rule thus suggests that it would be sensible for economists and other social scientists to reallocate some of their efforts away from the standard questions of labor force participation and weekly and annual workhours, and toward studying the determinants of days, hours, and daily schedules.

References

Abraham, Katharine, and Susan Houseman. 1993. *Job Security in America: Lessons from Germany.* Washington, DC: Brookings Institution.

Altonji, Joseph, and Christine Paxson. 1986. "Job Characteristics and Hours of Work," *Research in Labor Economics* 8: 1-55.

_____, and _____. 1992. "Labor Supply, Hours Constraints and Job Mobility," *Journal of Human Resources* 27: 256-78.

Appelbaum, Eileen, and Ronald Schettkat. 1990. "Determinants of Employment Developments: A Comparison of the United States and the Federal German Economies," *Labour and Society* 15: 13-31.

Ashenfelter, Orley, and Alan Krueger. 1994. "Estimates of the Economic Return to Schooling from a New Sample of Twins," *American Economic Review* 84: 1157-73.

Barzel, Yoram. 1973. "The Determination of Daily Hours and Wages," *Quarterly Journal of Economics* 87: 220-38.

Bell, Linda, and Richard Freeman. 1995. "Why Do Americans and Germans Work Different Hours?" In *Institutional Frameworks and Labor Market Performance*, Friedrich Buttler, Wolfgang Franz, Ronald Schettkat, and David Soskice, eds. London: Routledge.

Betancourt, Roger, and Christopher Clague. 1981. *Capital Utilization: A Theoretical and Empirical Analysis.* Cambridge: Cambridge University Press.

Biddle, Jeff, and Daniel Hamermesh. 1990. "Sleep and the Allocation of Time," *Journal of Political Economy* 98: 922-43.

_____, and Gary Zarkin. 1989. "Choices among Wage-Hours Packages: An Empirical Investigation of Labor Supply," *Journal of Labor Economics* 7: 415-37.

Bird, Edward, Johannes Schwarze, and Gert Wagner. 1994. "Wage Effects of the Move Toward Free Markets in East Germany," *Industrial and Labor Relations Review* 47: 390-400.

Blank, Rebecca. 1988. "Simultaneously Modeling the Supply of Weeks and Hours of Work among Female Household Heads," *Journal of Labor Economics* 6: 177-204.

Bresnahan, Timothy, and Valerie Ramey. 1994. "Output Fluctuations at the Plant Level," *Quarterly Journal of Economics* 109: 593-624.

Brown, C.V., E.J. Levin, P.J. Rosa, R.J. Ruffell, and D.T. Ulph. 1986 "Payment Systems, Demand Constraints and Their Implications for Research in Labour Supply." In *Unemployment, Search and Labour Supply*, Richard Blundell and Ian Walker, eds. Cambridge: Cambridge University Press.

Butcher, Kristin, and Anne Case. 1994. "The Effect of Sibling Sex Composition on Women's Education and Earnings," *Quarterly Journal of Economics* 109: 531-63.

Card, David. 1996. "The Effect of Unions on the Structure of Wages: A Longitudinal Analysis," *Econometrica* 64: forthcoming.

Christensen, Laurits, Dale Jorgenson, and Lawrence Lau. 1973. "Transcendental Logarithmic Production Frontiers," *Review of Economics and Statistics* 55: 28-45.

Cogan, John. 1980. "Labor Supply with Costs of Labor Market Entry." In *Female Labor Supply: Theory and Estimation*, James Smith, ed. Princeton, NJ: Princeton University Press.

Coleman, Mary, and John Pencavel. 1993. "Trends in Market Work Behavior of Women Since 1940," *Industrial and Labor Relations Review* 46: 653-76.

Curme, Michael, Barry Hirsch, and David McPherson. 1990. "Union Membership and Contract Coverage in the United States, 1983-1988," *Industrial and Labor Relations Review* 44: 5-33.

Ehrenberg, Ronald, and Paul Schumann. 1982. *Longer Hours or More Jobs?* Ithaca, NY: Cornell University Press.

Erdmann, Gerhard. 1957. *Die Entwicklung der deutschen Sozialgesetzgebung.* Göttingen: Musterschmidt.

Feldstein, Martin. 1967. "Specification of the Labour Input in the Aggregate Production Function," *Review of Economics Studies* 34: 638-55.

Florence, P. Sargant. 1924. *Economics of Fatigue and Unrest.* New York: Henry Holt.

Franz, Wolfgang, and Heinz König. 1986. "The Nature and Causes of Unemployment in the Federal Republic of Germany since the 1970s: An Empirical Investigation," *Economica* 53: S219-44.

Freeman, Richard, and James Medoff. 1982. "Substitution Between Production Labor and Other Inputs in Unionized and Non-Unionized Manufacturing," *Review of Economics and Statistics* 64: 220-33.

Gerlach, Knut, and Olaf Hübler. 1988. "Personalnebenkosten, Beschäftigtenzahl und Arbeitsstunden aus Neoklassischer und Institutionalistischer Sicht." In *Arbeitsmarkt und Beschäftigung*, Friedrich Buttler, Knut Gerlach and Rudi Schmiede, eds. Frankfurt: Campus.

_____, and _____. 1992. "Zuschläge zum Lohnpotential und Individuelle Arbeitslosigkeit." In *Mikro- und makroökonomische Aspekte der Arbeitslosigkeit*, Wolfgang Franz, ed. Nürnberg: Institut für Arbeitsmarkt- und Berufsforschung.

Ghez, Gilbert, and Gary Becker. 1975. *The Allocation of Time and Goods Over the Life Cycle.* New York: Columbia University Press.

Grant, James, and Daniel Hamermesh. 1981. "Labor Market Competition Among Youths, White Women and Others," *Review of Economics and Statistics* 63: 354-60.

Griliches, Zvi. 1969. "Capital-Skill Complementarity," *Review of Economics and Statistics* 51: 465-68.

Gustafsson, Siv, and Frank Stafford. 1992. "Childcare Subsidies and Labor Supply in Sweden," *Journal of Human Resources* 27: 204-30.

Hamermesh, Daniel. 1980. *Unemployment Insurance and the Older American*. Kalamazoo, MI: The W.E. Upjohn Institute.

_____. 1990. "Shirking or Productive Schmoozing? Wages and the Allocation of Time at Work," *Industrial and Labor Relations Review* 43: 121S-33S.

_____. 1993. *Labor Demand*. Princeton, NJ: Princeton University Press.

_____. 1995. "Policy Transferability and Hysteresis: Daily and Weekly Hours in the BRD and the US." In *Institutional Frameworks and Labor Market Performance*, Friedrich Buttler, Wolfgang Franz, Ronald Schettkat and David Soskice, eds. London: Routledge.

Hanoch, Giora. 1980a. "Hours and Weeks in the Theory of Labor Supply." In *Female Labor Supply: Theory and Estimation*, James Smith, ed. Princeton, NJ: Princeton University Press.

_____. 1980b. "A Multivariate Model of Labor Supply: Methodology and Estimation." In *Female Labor Supply: Theory and Estimation*, James Smith, ed. Princeton, NJ: Princeton University Press.

Hart, Robert. 1987. *Working Time and Employment*. Boston: Allen and Unwin.

_____, and Seiichi Kawasaki. 1988. "Payroll Taxes and Factor Demand," *Research in Labor Economics* 9: 257-85.

_____, and Peter McGregor. 1988. "The Returns to Labour Services in West German Manufacturing Industry," *European Economic Review* 32: 947-63.

Hedges, Janice Neipert, and Edward Sekscenski. 1979. "Workers on Late Shifts in a Changing Economy," *Monthly Labor Review* 102, 9: 14-22.

Hill, Martha. 1988. "Marital Stability and Spouses' Shared Time: A Multidisciplinary Hypothesis," *Journal of Family Issues* 9: 427-51.

Hunt, Jennifer. 1995. "The Effect of Unemployment Compensation on Unemployment Duration in Germany," *Journal of Labor Economics* 13: 88-120.

Killingsworth, Mark, and James Heckman. 1986. "Female Labor Supply: A Survey." In *Handbook of Labor Economics*, Orley Ashenfelter and Richard Layard, eds. Amsterdam: North-Holland.

König, Heinz, and Winfried Pohlmeier. 1988. "Employment, Labor Utilization and Procyclical Labor Productivity," *Kyklos* 41: 551-72.

_____, and _____. 1989. "Worksharing and Factor Prices: A Comparison of Three Flexible Functional Forms for Nonlinear Cost Schemes," *Journal of Institutional and Theoretical Economics* 145: 343-57.

Kostiuk, Peter. 1990. "Compensating Differentials for Shift Work," *Journal of Political Economy* 98: 1054-75.

Krishnan, Pramila. 1990. "The Economics of Moonlighting: A Double Self-selection Model," *Review of Economics and Statistics* 72: 361-7.

Laband, David, and Deborah Hendry Heinbuch. 1987. *Blue Laws*. Lexington, MA: Heath.

Mayshar, Joram, and Gary Solon. 1993. "Shift Work and the Business Cycle," American Economic Association, *Papers and Proceedings* 83: 224-28.

McLaughlin, Kenneth. 1991. "A Theory of Quits and Layoffs with Efficient Turnover," *Journal of Political Economy* 99: 1-29.

Melbin, Murray. 1987. *Night as Frontier*. New York: Free Press.

Mellor, Earl. 1986. "Shift Work and Flexitime: How Prevalent Are They?" *Monthly Labor Review* 109, 11: 14-21.

Organisation for Economic Co-operation and Development. 1992. *Employment Outlook*. Paris: OECD.

Owen, John. 1979. *Working Hours: An Economic Analysis*. Lexington, MA: Heath.

_____. 1986. *Working Lives: The American Work Force Since 1920*. Lexington, MA: Heath.

Palmer, Gladys. 1954. *Labor Mobility in Six Cities*. New York: Social Science Research Council.

Pashigian, B. Peter, and Brian Bowen. 1994. "The Rising Cost of Time of Females, the Growth of National Brands and the Supply of Retail Services," *Economic Inquiry* 32: 33-65.

Paxson, Christina, and Nachum Sicherman. 1996. "The Dynamics of Dual-Job Holding and Job Mobility," *Journal of Labor Economics* 14: forthcoming.

Poor, Riva. 1973. *4 Days, 40 Hours, and Other Forms of the Rearranged Workweek*. New York: New American Library.

Presser, Harriet. 1987. "Work Shifts of Full-Time Dual-Earner Couples: Patterns and Contrasts by Sex of Spouse," *Demography* 24: 99-112.

Schettkat, Ronald, and Susanne Fuchs. 1994. "Household Expenditures on Services and Service Employment in Germany: A Brief Investigation of Job Creation Potential." Unpublished paper, Wissenschaftszentrum Berlin.

Schor, Juliet. 1991. *The Overworked American*. New York: Basic Books.

Shapiro, Matthew. 1995. "Capital Utilization and the Marginal Premium for Work at Night." Unpublished paper, University of Michigan.

Sosin, Kim, and Loretta Fairchild. 1984. "Nonhomotheticity and Technological Bias in Production," *Review of Economics and Statistics* 66: 44-50.

Stafford, Frank. 1980. "Firm Size, Workplace Public Goods, and Worker Welfare." In *The Economics of Firm Size, Market Structure and Social Performance*, John Siegfried, ed. Washington: Federal Trade Commission.

_____, and Greg Duncan. 1980. "The Use of Time and Technology by Households in the United States," *Research in Labor Economics* 3: 335-75.

Szalai, Alexander. 1972. *The Use of Time: Daily Activities of Urban and Suburban populations in Twelve Countries*. The Hague: Mouton.

Triest, Robert. 1990. "The Effect of Income Taxation on Labor Supply in the United States," *Journal of Human Resources* 25: 491-525.

Weiss, Yoram. 1996. "Synchronization of Work Schedules," *International Economic Review* 37, forthcoming.

Welch, Finis. 1970. "Education in Production," *Journal of Political Economy* 78: 764-71.

Wilson, Paul. 1988. "Wage Variation Resulting from Staggered Work Hours," *Journal of Urban Economics* 24: 9-26.

Winston, Gordon. 1982. *The Timing of Economic Activities*. New York: Cambridge University Press.

INDEX

About the Institute

The W.E. Upjohn Institute for Employment Research is a nonprofit research organization devoted to finding and promoting solutions to employment-related problems at the national, state, and local level. It is an activity of the W.E. Upjohn Unemployment Trustee Corporation, which was established in 1932 to administer a fund set aside by the late Dr. W.E. Upjohn, founder of The Upjohn Company, to seek ways to counteract the loss of employment income during economic downturns.

The Institute is funded largely by income from the W.E. Upjohn Unemployment Trust, supplemented by outside grants, contracts, and sales of publications. Activities of the Institute are comprised of the following elements: (1) a research program conducted by a resident staff of professional social scientists; (2) a competitive grant program, which expands and complements the internal research program by providing financial support to researchers outside the Institute; (3) a publications program, which provides the major vehicle for the dissemination of research by staff and grantees, as well as other selected work in the field; and (4) an Employment Management Services division, which manages most of the publicly funded employment and training programs in the local area.

The broad objectives of the Institute's research, grant, and publication programs are to: (1) promote scholarship and experimentation on issues of public and private employment and unemployment policy; and (2) make knowledge and scholarship relevant and useful to policymakers in their pursuit of solutions to employment and unemployment problems.

Current areas of concentration for these programs include: causes, consequences, and measures to alleviate unemployment; social insurance and income maintenance programs; compensation; workforce quality; work arrangements; family labor issues; labor-management relations; and regional economic development and local labor markets.